ROAD TR
AND TRANSPORT
IN GLOUCESTERSHIRE
1722–1822

Extracts from the *Gloucester Journal*
edited and introduced by

NICHOLAS HERBERT

ALAN SUTTON &
GLOUCESTERSHIRE COUNTY LIBRARY
1985

The County Library Series is published jointly by Alan Sutton
Publishing Limited and Gloucestershire County Library. All
correspondence relating to the series should be addressed to:

Alan Sutton Publishing Limited
30 Brunswick Road
Gloucester GL1 1JJ

First published 1985

BRITISH LIBRARY CATALOGUING IN PUBLICATION DATA

Road travel and transport in Gloucestershire.
  1. Transportation, Automotive—England—Gloucestershire—
  History—18th century 2. Transportation, Automotive—England—
  Gloucestershire—History—19th century
  I. Herbert, N.M.
  388.3'09424'1   HE5664.G/

ISBN 0-86299-235-4

Typesetting and origination by
Alan Sutton Publishing Limited
Photoset Palatino 10/12
Printed in Great Britain

Contents

	Page
List of illustrations	iv
Preface	v
Acknowledgements	vii
Abbreviations	viii
Chapter I: THE IMPROVEMENT OF THE ROADS	1

Chapter II: INNS
Town Inns and Country Inns	21
Rival Inns (1): Andoversford versus Frogmill	31
Rival Inns (2): Rodborough versus Frocester	34
'Your Humble Servant' – An Obeisance of Innkeepers	40

Chapter III: COACHES
'Performed if God Permit' – The Main Routes	44
The Mail Coaches	57
Rival Coaches – The 'Union' versus 'Masters'	62

Chapter IV: CARRIERS
Packhorse and Wagon	69
Serving the Clothing Country	79
The Lechlade Route	84
The Carriers and the Turnpikes	89

Chapter V: TRAVELLERS
Tradesmen and Others	96
Rogues and Vagabonds	104
Showmen and Entertainers	115

Chapter VI: THE DANGERS OF TRAVEL
Robbery with Violence	121
Road Accidents	127
Bad Weather	134

| Chapter VII: THE SEVERN PASSAGES | 137 |
| Index of Places and Subjects | 148 |

List of Illustrations

For permission to reproduce material in their possession I am most grateful to the following: Avon County Reference Library, Bristol; the British Library; Cheltenham Art Gallery and Museum; Gloucester Divisional Library; Gloucestershire Record Office; Luton Museum and Art Gallery; Messrs. Rickerbys, solicitors, of Cheltenham.

Page

Over causeway, Gloucester. Detail of an engraving by Samuel and Nathaniel Buck, 1734 (Glouc. Library) 4

Halfpenny bridge, Lechlade. Engraving by G. Cooke, 1815 (Glouc. Library) 8

Roadmaking. Etchings by J.H. Pyne, from *Microcosm; or a picturesque delineation of the arts, agriculture, manufactures, etc., of Great Britain*, 1806 (Luton Museum) 12

Turnpike on the London road, Cheltenham. Painting by G. Colley, in possession of Rickerbys, solicitors, Cheltenham 14

Stone quarries on the River Avon, near Bristol. Aquatint by Ibbetson, Laporte, and Hassell, from *Picturesque Guide to Bath, Bristol Hot-wells, and the adjacent country*, 1793 (Avon Library) 18

The Bell inn, Gloucester. Engraving by George Virtue, from R. Philip, *Life and Times of the Revd. George Whitefield*, 3rd edn. 1842 (Glos. Record Office) . . 22

Cheltenham High Street. Painting in possession of Cheltenham Museum and Art Gallery 24

Advertisement for the Ram inn, Cirencester (Glos. Record Office) . . . 28

Cirencester market place. Engraving by J. Burden, 1804 (Glos. Record Office) 32

Wagon by the Swan inn, Tewkesbury (Glos. Record Office) 36

Coach and carrier's advertisements, from the *Gloucester Journal*, 1 Apr. 1729 (Glouc. Library) 45

Tewkesbury High Street (Glos. Record Office) 48

Coach advertisement, from S.Y. Griffith, *New Historical Description of Cheltenham*, 1826 (Glouc. Library) 52

Mail coach advertisements, from the *Gloucester Journal*, 21 Nov. 1785 (Glouc. Library) 58

The Bull and Mouth inn, London. Engraving from a drawing by T.H. Shepherd, from J. Elmes, *London and its Environs in the 19th Century*, 1829 (British Library) 64

Packhorses at Avening. Engraving from R. Bigland, *Collections Relative to the County of Gloucester*, vol. i, 1791 (Glos. Record Office) 72

Wagons. Etchings by J.H. Pyne, from *Microcosm* (Luton Museum) . . . 76

Carriers' advertisement, from Griffith, *op.cit.* (Glouc. Library) 80

Wagon passing Millbank Penitentiary. Engraving from a drawing by T.H. Shepherd, from J. Elmes, *Metropolitan Improvements; or London in the Nineteenth Century*, 1828 (British Library) 86

Timber wagon in Tewkesbury. Engraving by G. Rowe (Glouc. Library) . . 90

Advertisement for the *Gloucester Journal*, c. 1738 (Glouc. Library, Glos. Colln. NV 26. 1) 100

Extract from account book of the Revd. Charles Coxwell, 1777–9 (Glos. Record Office, D 269B/F13) 106

Market traffic in Westgate Street, Gloucester. Detail of an engraving from a drawing by W.H. Bartlett, from J. Britton, *Picturesque Antiquities of the English Cities*, 1836 (Glouc. Library) 112

Traffic on Westgate bridge, Gloucester. Drawing of 1792 (taken from a photo in Glos. Record Office) 124

The New Inn, Gloucester. Engraving from a drawing by W.H. Bartlett, from Britton, *op. cit.* (Glouc. Library) 128

Stagecoaches. Etchings by J.H. Pyne, from *Microcosm* (Luton Museum) . . 132

Advertisement for Aust Passage House (Avon Library) 140

Beachley Passage House. Detail from an innkeeper's advertisement (Avon Library) 144

The New Passage. Aquatint by Ibbetson, Laporte, and Hassell, from *Picturesque Guide* (Avon Library) 146

Preface

For those embarking on research into the social history of Gloucester-shire in the modern period the *Gloucester Journal* can be an object of both delight and despondency. Published every week from 1722 for a region that included the whole of the ancient county, the newspaper provides an always valuable, often essential, but dauntingly time-consuming source of information on a wide range of historical subjects. Into its rich deposits some have been content to sink shafts at random, while others have quarried more systematically along a particular seam, but much remains unexploited. The object of this book is to make more readily available some of the evidence to be found in the first 100 years of the *Journal* for just one historical topic – road travel and transport in Gloucestershire.

For some aspects of this topic, for example the coach-services and the carriers, the paper is the premier source during the 18th century. For other aspects it is only one among a number of important sources: for example, in the study of the efforts to improve the condition of the roads (the subject of my first chapter) many other sources – the records of the turnpike trusts, the writings of contemporary diarists and topographers, maps, and the evidence surviving on the ground – have an equal or greater role to play. There are, too, other aspects which it would be superfluous to try and illustrate from the pages of the *Journal*: there are, for example, many notices in the paper which relate to the organisation and administration of the turnpike trusts, but I decided against including that as a separate section because it is a subject that can be more fully and more appropriately studied from the surviving turnpike minutes and accounts. In general, however, road travel and transport is one of the topics of the history of Georgian Gloucestershire for which the *Gloucester Journal* is an essential source.

The history of the newspaper itself has been related in detail by Roland Austin (in the *Bicentenary Gloucester Journal* of 8 April, 1922), and it need only be briefly summarised here. The *Gloucester Journal*, one of the leading English provincial newspapers, was founded at Gloucester in 1722 by the partnership of Robert Raikes and William Dicey, who were already proprietors of a Northampton paper. Raikes became the sole owner in 1725 and carried on the paper with vigour and success until his death in 1757, when he was succeeded by his son Robert. The younger Raikes used the paper as a vehicle for publicising and furthering his philanthropic aims, particularly the Sunday School movement, but he was nevertheless a practical and successful newspaperman and the *Journal* had no serious rival in the county while the 18th century lasted. Raikes sold the paper in 1802 to David Walker, owner of the *Hereford Journal*. Walker's two sons joined him in the business in 1816 and one of them David Mowbray Walker, remained owner and editor until his death in 1871. The *Journal* passed into the same ownership as a daily Gloucester paper, the *Citizen*, in 1879.

During the period covered by the extracts in this book the *Journal* circulated throughout Gloucestershire and well beyond its boundaries, extending into most of the neighbouring counties and – along the routes of communication that Gloucester commanded – far into South Wales. Like most of its contemporaries, its news columns were filled mainly with extracts from the London papers, local news and comment occupying during most of the period only a paragraph or two on the third page. Local advertisements and various kinds of public announcements, however, appear in growing volume and by the early years of the 19th century occupied about three-fifths of the space. It is those which are so valuable as a source for the social and economic history of Gloucestershire and which supply the great majority of the extracts published here.

I have taken as the basic catchment area the county of Gloucestershire as it existed up to 1974, only occasionally straying down some of the main roads which led out of the county. The bulk of the material will, however, be seen to relate to the middle part of the old county, extending roughly from Lechlade across to Mitcheldean and from Tewkesbury down to Tetbury. That is the region which a paper published in Gloucester naturally tended to give the fullest coverage. As regards the terminal date of 1822, this has no particular significance in the history of road transport, but was chosen because it completes a neat 100 years. One thing very certain is that the extracts included here are only a very small, though I hope fairly representative, sample of the mass of information that the *Journal* has to offer on the subject for that region in that period.

The extracts are given verbatim with the original spelling and punctuation (and the contemporary usage of initial capitals for common nouns); any omissions or curtailments are indicated by dots in the usual way. No attempt has been made to reproduce the often very complicated typography of the newspaper, which used a variety of sizes and styles of type; but I have kept at least something of the original appearance of the advertisements and announcements as regards the layout and the use of capitals for emphasis. One general point that will help with the understanding of the extracts is that 'this city' refers, of course, to Gloucester.

Acknowledgements

The bulk of the items printed in this book were found over a period of some twelve years while searching the *Gloucester Journal* in the course of my work for the Victoria History of Gloucestershire, which is a joint project of the Gloucestershire County Council and London University. For many of the extracts for the period up to 1760, however, I am indebted to Michael Handford, a historian of Gloucestershire's canals, who generously made his notes available to me. The bound sets of the *Journal* are a much prized item in the fine local history collection at the Gloucester Divisional Library, Brunswick Road, Gloucester, and I am most grateful to successive librarians (currently Mr. G.R. Hiatt) and their staffs for providing access to them. Jill Voyce and Dr. Steven Blake gave valuable help with finding suitable illustrations. My manuscript was expertly typed by Margaret Collier.

N.M. Herbert
1985

Abbreviations Used in the Introductory Notes to the Chapters

Bennett, *Tewkes.*	James Bennett, *The History of Tewkesbury* (Tewkesbury, 1830)
Counsel, *Gloucester*	G.W. Counsel, *The History and Description of the City of Gloucester* (Gloucester, 1829)
Defoe, *Tour Through the Whole Island*	Daniel Defoe, *A Tour Through the Whole Island of Great Britain* (Penguin edn., ed. P. Rogers, 1971)
Fisher, *Stroud*	Paul Hawkins Fisher, *Notes and Recollections of Stroud, Gloucestershire* (2nd edn., Stroud, 1891)
G.J.	*The Gloucester Journal*
Glos. R.O.	Gloucestershire Record Office
Glos. Turnpike Roads	*Gloucestershire Turnpike Roads* (Glos. Record Office 'Signal' Series, 1973)
Rudder, *New History*	Samuel Rudder, *A New History of Gloucestershire* (Cirencester, 1779)
V.C.H. Glos	*The Victoria History of Gloucestershire* (O.U.P., for the Institute of Historical Research), Vol. VII (1981); X (1972); XI (1976)

CHAPTER ONE

The Improvement of the Roads

The period covered by the extracts from the *Gloucester Journal* in this book saw a gradual revolution in the condition and appearance of the roads of Gloucestershire. Widened, straightened, resurfaced, and in many places replaced by new-built sections of road, the historic pattern of main highways was transformed out of all recognition. The extracts printed in this first chapter illustrate some of the various aspects of that process as it was reported on, publicised, and actively promoted in the columns of the county's principal newspaper.

The agents of the transformation in the state of the roads, the turnpike trusts with their powers to finance road improvement by the levying of tolls and raising loans, first made their appearance in the county in 1698 with an Act of Parliament for the repair of the first few miles of the two alternative London roads from Gloucester city, up Crickley hill and up Birdlip hill. It was not, however, until 1726 that other major routes out of the city, towards Bristol, South Wales, and Hereford, were brought under the system, and not until the middle years of the 18th century, when Acts were secured for various routes over the Cotswolds centred on the towns of Tetbury, Cirencester, and Stow-on-the-Wold, that something like a turnpike network began to appear (For a map with the dates of the principal turnpikes, see *Glos. Turnpike Roads*, no. 7). When first introduced in England the new system of financing road repairs was hailed enthusiastically as the answer to the problems so long endured by travellers. Defoe in his *Tour Through the Whole Island* (pp. 429–44) noted many examples of roads where rapid improvement had been brought about by the turnpike trusts, including one of those covered by Gloucester's 1698 Act, which he mentions as '. . . the road from Birdlip Hill to Gloucester, formerly a terrible place for poor carriers and travellers out of Wales, &c. but now repaired very well.'

In Gloucestershire as elsewhere, however, the early optimism was not justified. A lack of energy on the part of the trustees and some financial mismanagement prevented any very obvious improvement during the early years of the system and led to widespread disillusionment and hostility among road-users, manifested most dramatically in the violent

1

destruction of many of the turnpike gates. The events at Bristol in 1749 were among the most spectacular of such outbreaks, but the *Journal* reports other incidents in Gloucestershire and neighbouring counties throughout the early years of the trusts (nos. 1–2; and see *G.J.* 18 Aug. 1730; 22 June, 26 Oct. 1731; 30 Sept. 1735). The gates around Gloucester were destroyed in May 1734 by an armed mob which then stormed into the city shouting 'Blood for Blood' and 'Down with the Turnpikes' (*Glos. Notes and Queries*, iv, pp. 493–4). The following month in an open letter to the *Journal*, outlining proposals for improving on the sorry performance of the Gloucester–Hereford trust, in which he was the principal investor, Henry Guise mentioned that the turnpike at Over bridge on that road had 'several times of late been destroy'd upon Account (as it is given out) of the Badness of the Roads leading from Newent and Huntley to the said Turnpike' (*G.J.* 11 June 1734). The imposition of tolls was in itself likely to annoy the local road-user and lead to incidents such as that recorded at one of the gates on the Stroud–Tetbury road in 1758, the first year it came under a turnpike trust (no. 5). That annoyance was compounded as time passed and the road-user could see little return for his money. Even in later years when the turnpike gate had become a familiar feature of the roadside scenery it remained a focus for popular discontent, the customary badinage between traveller and gate-keeper occasionally deteriorating into something more serious (no. 13; Chapter IV, no. 131).

Dissatisfaction at the poor results of the turnpike system was reflected at a different level in the grumblings about the condition of the roads that are a regular theme of writers on the county throughout the 18th century. As late as the 1770s when Samuel Rudder took to the roads in pursuit of material for his county history there were still some serious problems for him to record, particularly on the roads which cross the heavy clay of the Vale. Of part of the Gloucester–Bristol road, one of the major highways of the county and a turnpike since 1726, Rudder wrote '. . . surely there cannot be a more infamous turnpike-road . . . for, incredible as it may seem, the writer of this account, in the winter of 1776, saw a chaise mired in it, about half a mile from the Swan inn (in Wheatenhurst), and was there told, that a horse had like to have been smothered in the same place two days before, but was luckily saved by some persons coming accidentally to the poor animal's assistance. Several causes operate to this evil; the scarcity of stone, the remissness of the commissioners; and the total ignorance of the surveyor' (*New History*, p. 813).

Gradually, however, more energetic and efficient management by the turnpike commissioners, the adoption of new road-building techniques, and the introduction of better road-building materials began to have a discernible impact on the network of main roads of the county. Most of the engineering works carried out by the trusts were on a small, undramatic scale but are often still readily apparent to the motorist today. A stretch of road ascending a steep hill by means of a bend or series of bends is often the creation of the local trust and sometimes the original packhorse road that it replaced can still be seen, taking a more direct and much steeper course. Good examples are on the old Gloucester–Bath road up Frocester hill, where the new piece of road was built in about 1783 (Chapter II, no. 47), and on the road from the Chalford valley up towards Bisley just above Chalford church. 'Lowering' a hill by making a cutting in an existing road was another method of easing a gradient and is well illustrated by the improvement made in 1820 on the Gloucester–Chepstow road where it leaves Newnham (no. 20). A short new stretch of road bypassing a difficult bend or a constricted way between old cottages is often clearly identifiable, as on part of the old Stroud–Cirencester turnpike just north of Minchinhampton, where the new piece of road was built in 1783 (G.J. 10 Feb.).

More striking improvements were the new bridges provided at crossings of rivers or streams. The substantial, four-arch stone bridge built by the Bath–Cirencester trust in 1775 to carry their road across a narrow valley on the south side of Tetbury town is a particularly good object lesson in the improvements brought by the trusts, for on the stream beneath it there still survives the old packhorse bridge and ford which it replaced. Halfpenny bridge built across the Thames at Lechlade in 1792 by the trustees of the Burford–Highworth road is another example. Daniel Harris, the architect responsible, may not have been a man of any great eminence in his profession – he carried it on in conjunction with the post of keeper of the Oxford gaol – but his elegant arch at Lechlade is one of the most pleasing creations of the turnpike era in Gloucestershire (no. 14; and see H. Colvin, *Biographical Dict. of Brit. Architects*, 1978, p. 391).

As their finances improved and more engineering expertise became available to them the turnpike trusts began to redraw parts of the map of the road-system of the county by building some completely new roads. The Gloucester–Bath road along the Nailsworth valley which figures in a later section of this book (Chapter II, nos. 43–8) was one of the earliest of such ventures, and that particular region of the county, the valleys centred on Stroud, was one that was to have its road-system revolutionised by the trusts. The old roads in that region, which crossed the tops of the hills or else wound along the valley sides like the physical

Over bridge and causeway, Gloucester, in 1734. A carrier's wagon has just passed Over turnpike, and a string of packhorses is coming in on the Ledbury road.

embodiment of contour lines, were replaced by a series of new routes following the valley bottoms. By 1820 a man travelling from Stroud towards Gloucester, Cheltenham, Cirencester, or Nailsworth would leave the town on a road that had not existed in his grandfather's day. In the county as a whole road-building reached a crescendo of activity at the end of the period covered by these extracts, in the 1820s. That decade saw, among other projects, the final strands of the new Stroud valley system; new roads that Cheltenham needed to match its enhanced status, including a new Bath route by Shurdington and Painswick (no. 22) and a new Cirencester route along the Churn valley; and new bridges over the Severn at the Haw and the Mythe, built as parts of two rival new London to Hereford routes (*G.J.* 28 Oct. 1822).

An important factor in the major improvement of the roads in the late 18th and early 19th centuries was the availability of more satisfactory road-building material. The local stones of north Gloucestershire, the oolitic limestone of the hills and the grey lias limestone quarried in the Vale and on Severnside, were too soft and friable to make a durable surface, and it was only in the late years of the 18th century that the trusts of the region began to go further afield for harder stone to make the top dressing on their roads. The harder stone was brought in particular from quarries on the Bristol Avon and on the Wye near Chepstow and Tintern and it became one of the principal cargoes carried up the Severn by the trows and other vessels (nos. 17, 23; and see T. Rudge, *Agriculture of Glos.*, 1807, pp. 333–4). The Gloucester–Cheltenham turnpike, for example, began using Bristol stone in the mid 1780s to supplement that from its local sources at Churchdown hill and Cooper's hill (Glos. R.O., D 204/1/1).

For the 18th-century Englishman the state of the roads was a regular topic of conversation and complaint. Methods of improving the roads were widely debated among the wealthier classes, and the turnpike trustees and the parish highway surveyors, who remained responsible for the minor roads, were subjected to the scrutiny and advice of pressure groups of local gentry. These groups, which raised funds for the prosecution of negligent road authorities and supplied information on road-building techniques, are represented below by notices issued in 1756 (nos. 3–4). Also to be found in the *Journal* are a 'Vale of Evesham Road Club', formed in 1792 for an area that included Evesham, Pershore, Tewkesbury, and Winchcombe (*G.J.* 3, 17 Sept., 22 Oct., 19 Nov. 1792; and see Bennett, *Tewkes.*, p. 281; and *Glos. Turnpike Roads*, no. 18) and a prosecution society that operated in 1813 for the roads of the Cheltenham area (*G.J.* 1 Mar. 1813).

The *Journal* itself was an important vehicle for encouraging improvements and providing advice to road-builders. The younger Robert Raikes regarded his position as proprietor of a major provincial newspaper as one that carried with it a duty to promote the economic well-being, as well as the moral improvement, of the region it served. Two editorials touching on the question of the roads printed below (nos. 7, 16) give a good idea of the tone adopted by the paper on a wide range of public matters during Raikes's long period as editor.

One theme that emerges strongly from the advertisements, letters, and public notices on the subject of the roads in the *Journal* is the importance of road transport for the livelihood of individuals and communities. The continuance, improvement, or diversion of a particular route could be a matter of great concern to the inns which stood on it (see Chapter II, nos. 41–8); to individuals with a direct financial stake in it, including those who had invested money in it on security of the tolls, the lessees of the tolls, and the surveyors, clerks, and others employed by the trustees; to tradesmen and shopkeepers for whom the passing trade it brought had significance; and to the economy in general of the towns through which it passed. People interested in some particular road frequently came forward in the columns of the newspaper to proclaim its advantages over rival routes or to publicise some recent improvement. Alternative routes that the traveller into South Wales could take after leaving Gloucester were assiduously promoted by the innkeepers of Ross-on-Wye on one hand and of Mitcheldean on the other, while Ross was also the rival of Ledbury for the traffic from Gloucester to Hereford (nos. 8–9, 15). The changes in the road-system of the Stroud valleys were of great significance to the small market towns of that area. Nailsworth people would have been among the main supporters of the new Gloucester–Bath road of 1780, which proved to be a major influence in the growth of that place from a group of loosely-connected hamlets into a small town. A notice issued in 1813 (no. 19) reflects the disquiet among Minchinhampton inhabitants about the new Chalford valley road (built the following year) which threatened to take away from their town the main route from Stroud to Cirencester and London.

No. 19 also reminds us that another pressure group which might oppose or support plans for a new road were the owners of land through which it was to run. In the case of the Chalford valley road the opposition was pre-empted by the trustees, who 'assembled a large body of laborers, who commenced their operations in the night; and had levelled all the hedges and other obstructions on a considerable portion of the intended road, before the millowners and landowners arose in the morning; and before any contracts had been made for the land over which it was to pass' (Fisher, *Stroud*, p. 152).

1 *22 September 1730*

Whereas the Turnpike erected at Codrington-Ash in the County of Gloucester, was, on Saturday the 29th Day of August last past, pull'd down: These are therefore to give Notice, that if any Person concern'd in pulling down the said Turnpike, will discover the rest of his Accomplices, so that they may be apprehended and brought to Justice, (he) shall for such Discovery, receive of the Treasurer of the said Turnpike Twenty Guineas, upon the Conviction of any such Person or Persons for the said Crime.

2 *8 August 1749*

Letter from Bristol, August 2.

"Yesterday about the Middle of the Day the Somersetshire Men destroy'd the Turn-Pikes on that Side, and afterwards came into the City; they said their Number amounted to 900 Men, but some, who have seen them, believe them to be about 200. Upon their being kept out at Redcliffe-Gate, they went to the Turnpike leading to Brislington, in the Road to Bath; and, whilst they were cutting that down, the City-Constable, headed by some of the Commissioners, and followed by Sailors, went to them, dispers'd them, and took and brought in 25 of them, some wounded very much, and one, we hear, is since dead of his Wounds. We next expect the Gloucestershire Colliers, who have been preparing Fire-Arms and other Weapons ever since Two o'Clock this Morning, and who give out that they will rescue the above Prisoners now in Newgate."

The Contents of the above Letter are confirm'd by other Intelligence receiv'd and dated from Bristol as this Day; but we have no Account of any other Skirmishes happening: All that we learn further is, that the City of Bristol is under the most terrible Apprehensions, that Trade is there entirely at a Stand, and that the Colliers continued resolute in their Intentions.

They write from Wotton-Underedge, that the Colliers had cut down the Pike at Yeat, and also the large Elm that had stood there for 100 Years, which they burnt Yesterday in the Afternoon.

3 *9 March 1756*

Whereas the High-ways leading from a Place called the Broad-oak, in the County of Hereford, through the several Parishes of St. Wenards, Skenfrith, Landilo, Lanferring, Landevy, Landilo-Perthony, or by whatever other Name and Names the above Parishes are called, are at present in a founderous, dangerous Manner, owing to the Indolence and Neglect of the inhabitants; This is therefore to give Notice, That there is a

Halfpenny bridge at Lechlade, built in 1792 by the trustees of the Burford and Highworth turnpike road.

sufficient Sum of Money raised towards carrying on a Prosecution against the Inhabitants of the above Parishes, if they do not forthwith cut down their Hedges, open and scour the Ditches, make and mend the said High-ways: And it is here desired the several Surveyors will take Notice, That for almost every Neglect of their's they forfeit the Sum of Five Pounds; and they may depend it shall be levied if they neglect Duty. It is amazing any Person whatever should be negligent in an Affair of such Publick Utility. This is a great Road leading from several Parts of South-Wales to Ross, Hereford, Worcester, Glocester, &c. so that every Land-holder, every Landlord, must think it, if they think at all, their Interest to be strenuous in an Affair of such Importance.

23 March 1756

Whereas an Advertisement was published in this Paper of the 9th Instant, concerning the High Roads leading from Ross to Abergavenny; the Inhabitants and Surveyors of the Parishes there mentioned, and of all other Parishes on the said Road are again desired to observe the said Advertisement; and that, when they set about mending the said Roads, they would not make poor, narrow Causeways, just under the Hedges, as usual, and of great Stones, but would raise their Work in the Middle of the Road, that there may be a Fall for the Water on each Side; and that too they will, with proper Hammers, &c. break the Stones small, and throw Earth over all; which Method will make the Roads good for several Years. Remember your Hedges and Drains!

N.B. The Subscribers have given Orders to Two Attorneys to carry on the Prosecution in Case of Neglect.

4   *20 April 1756*

To the AUTHOR, &c.

SIR,

To prevent any more Taxes on Travelling in Glocestershire, a voluntary Subscription is talked of for the Care of the Roads or Highways, that they are repaired and kept in Repair upon the following Plan, viz.

An Annual Subscription of 5s. payable on Lady-Day; That the Subscribers, who send Instructions for an Information, &c. are desired to send to Mr. *John Doe*, Attorney at, &c. a particular Account of the Road intended to be indicted, the Parish or Hamlet where it lies, and the Names of the Surveyors of such Parish or Hamlet; who is immediately to give Notice to such Surveyors to amend or repair such Roads before the next Assizes to be holden for Glocestershire; That, in case such Road be not amended or repaired, and sufficient Reasons be not given for the Neglect or Refusal, the same will be indicted at the said Assizes, and an Information will be brought in the Crown-office against the Surveyors for Neglect of Duty, &c.; That the Notices for repairing the Roads be given at any Time between Lady-day and Midsummer, but at no other Time; That no Information or Indictment be carried on or commenced but with the Consent of the Committee; and what is done by the Committee shall be binding to all Subscribers; The Subscribers to have a Meeting Once a Quarter, to make Rules and Orders, and to chuse a Committee, &c. N.B. Great Care will be taken that there is no Indictment, &c. 'till after the Surveyors have had the most reasonable Notice.

5 *19 September 1758*

Whereas a Person unknown did, on Tuesday the Fifth Instant, beat and assault George Hicks, the Keeper of the Turnpike-Gate at a Place called Woeful-Dean Bottom, on the Road from Hampton to Tetbury, and forcibly passed through the said Gate, without paying the Toll appointed by Act of Parliament to be paid; The Commissioners of the said Turnpike, therefore, hereby offer a Reward of One Guinea, over and above what is allowed by the said Act, to any one who shall discover the said Person: The same to be paid by their Clerk, Mr James Dalby, of Tetbury, immediately on Conviction of the Offender.

6 *28 August 1759*

Notice is hereby given,

That such able Men, who are used to dig Stones, or work upon Turnpike-Roads, may be employed, bringing with them a Pick-Axe and Shovel, on Monday the 3d Day of September next, upon the New Turnpike-Road from Frocester-Hill, leading to the Town of Tetbury, in the County of Glocester, at 14d. per Day, 'till the 12th Day of November next, by me,
JOSEPH PARRY, Surveyor.

7 *6 June 1763*

The gentlemen of Carmarthenshire, emulating the zeal for the publick good which has distinguished their neighbours of Breconshire, last week set on foot the construction of a great turnpike road through their county; in which work above a hundred hands, we are told, are now employed. Good roads may be justly ranked amongst the first measures to be pursued for the enrichment of a country: by facilitating communications they may be said in effect to reduce the distances of places. Estates will, by this means, be brought nearer to the markets, and the conveyance of corn and other commodities being easier, the farmer will be inspired with greater industry in the improvement of his lands, lime and other kinds of manure* will be more readily distributed over the country, and the landlord will perceive his demesnes annually to increase in value. Thus will good roads reciprocally advantage the whole community; and the gentlemen of Carmarthenshire, as well as Breconshire, be held forth as objects of imitation throughout that principality. And who can tell, but a good road to Carmarthen may invite the Goddess Concord to take a trip thither: there may she exert her genial influence, and extirpate faction, the bane of every good, which has so long distracted that ancient borough, and banished from it every blessing of society; then, and then only, may we expect to see industry, and with her commerce, resume her seat at Carmarthen; again, as formerly, the emporium of Wales.

* No waggon which carries corn, &c. to the Bristol market returns home empty; but all load back with the soil, ashes, &c. of the town, which is found to pay the back-carriage extremely well, by the great improvement which the land receives from such manure.

8   *26 September 1768*

TO THE

PRINTER of the GLOCESTER JOURNAL.

SIR,   Ledbury, Aug. 13.
Having lately seen an Advertisement in your Paper from a Ross Corre-spondent, who attempts to recommend himself and the Use of his Post-Chaise to the Public, on the Ross Road between Hereford and Glocester, by saying, "That the Road from Glocester to Hereford through Ledbury is farther by four Miles than through Ross, and a dismal Country!" I am induced not only to set forth the real Truth, in Gratitude to many Gentlemen who have been very assiduous in compleating the Roads between Hereford and Glocester through Ledbury, but also in Justice to the Ledbury Landlords, who are furnished with extreme good Post-Chaises, able Horses, and careful Drivers, upon the most reasonable Terms, and accomodate the Nobility, Gentlemen, and Tradesmen, in the most obliging and genteel Manner: I think it also, necessary to observe to the Public, that the Gentlemen who have made it their Object to amend the Roads near Ledbury, have lately expended Two Thousand Pounds to make it spacious and complete, and continue, at great Expence, to keep them so: And as I am fully convinced, as well by ocular Demonstration as otherwise, that your Ross Correspondent is mistaken in his Notions, not only with Respect to the Goodness of the Road and the Pleasantness of the Country through Ledbury (which will appear to an impartial Observer to be exceedingly pleasant and agreeable, much more level than through Ross, and with Respect to the Distance, equally the same, and may be travelled in much less Time than through Ross): I therefore desire, Mr. Raikes, that you will insert in your next Paper the State of the three principal Roads from your City of Glocester into South-Wales, as well through Ross as through Ledbury and Monmouth, as hereunder truly set forth, without any Variation, which will greatly oblige many of your Readers, and particularly,

Your humble Servant,
A Friend to the Publick.

11

Roadmaking in the early 19th century.

From BRECON to GLOCESTER,

Thro' Ledbury.	Miles	Thro' Ross.	Miles	Thro' Monmouth.	Miles
To the Hay	15	To the Hay	15	To Abergavenny	20
Bredwardine		Bredwardine		Monmouth	16
Bridge	8	Bridge	8	Dean	16
Hereford	12	Hereford	12	Glocester	14
Ledbury	16	Ross	14		————
Glocester	16	Glocester	18	Post-Miles	66
	————		————		
Post-Miles	67	Post-Miles	67		

N.B. It there be any Difference in the Distance through Ross and through Ledbury, it appears, upon a just Mensuration, to be in Favour of the Ledbury Road about three Fourths of a Mile.

9 *19 February 1770*

ROSS

These are to acquaint the Nobility, Gentry, and others travelling between Glocester, Hereford, and South-Wales, That the Road between Glocester and Ross is now made very good, and will be constantly under Reparation 'till the same shall be made exceeding good, and is much the pleasantest Road from Glocester to Hereford: And whereas it has been customary to charge 18 Miles from Ross to Glocester, We, whose Names are under written, do purpose to run the same at 15 Miles.

Neat Post-Chaises, able Horses, and careful Drivers, to be had on the shortest Notice, with genteel Usage from

Their humble Servants,
GEORGE ROBERTS, the King's-Head.
JOHN BALL, the King's-Arms.
HUMP. LYCETT, the Swan and Falcon.

10 *9 February 1778*

Turnpike Road from Cirencester to Lansdown.

All Persons willing to contract for the easing, lowering, and rendering more commodious, the Hills called Frizen-Hill, and Lillyput-Hill, on the said Road, near the Monument upon Lansdown, are desired to send in their Plans and Estimates, on or before the 1st of March next, to James Ludlow, Attorney, in Chipping-Sodbury.

11 *13 September 1784*

An Advertisement lately appearing in the papers, stating that the road from Monmouth to Glocester, through Ross, was nearer than through Coleford and Mitcheldean; a very accurate admeasurement has been taken

13

Turnpike gate on the London road, Cheltenham, c. 1835.

by me, Thomas Pinnell, Land Surveyor, of Glocester, by which it appears, that from Monmouth to Ross is 10 miles and five furlongs, and from Ross to Glocester (according to the mile stones) 16 miles, making 26 miles and five furlongs, that from Monmouth to Mitcheldean (through the new cut in the Forest, avoiding the hills) 14 miles, and from Mitcheldean to the seven mile stone at Huntley on the road to Glocester (and which road has been considerably improved by a new cut through the hill near Mitcheldean) four miles and one furlong. The difference, therefore, in favour of the Mitcheldean road, is one mile and four furlongs.

THOMAS PINNELL

12   *8 May 1786*

Whereas a New Road is now making between Cheltenham and Frogmill, through the parish of Dowdeswell, by which the distance between Glocester and Frogmill will be the same as through the heavy vale, and up the long and steep hills of Crickley and Chatcomb, now used, – It is proposed by the Trustees of the said road between Glocester and Cheltenham to take up the sum of Two Thousand Pounds immediately, in order to put the said road into perfect repair, to join the road now making from Cheltenham through Dowdeswell to Frogmill, by which there will be no material hill to ascend, and which will render this road in every respect the most preferable line to London.

Whoever is or are willing to advance the said sum, or any part of it, at 5 per cent. (for which the Interest will be regularly paid) are desired to apply to Mr. Edward Driver, in Glocester, Clerk to the Trustees.
Glocester, April 27.

13   *7 September 1789*

It is recommended to a certain turnpike man, not many miles from Tetbury, on the Bath road, to be more civil, and less imposing to gentlemen travelling through his gate. The inserter of this paragraph has, himself, in common with many others, experienced both insolence and imposition from the person alluded to; and he hopes this gentle admonition will operate as a caution to him in his future conduct, which otherwise will endanger a prosecution he but too justly merits.

14   *6 August 1792*

To Builders, Masons, and Carpenters.

Notice is hereby given, that the Trustees, appointed in or by virtue of an act of Parliament passed in the last session, "For repairing, widening, turning, and altering the road leading from the town of Burford, in the county of Oxford, to Leachlade, in the county of Glocester; and for making a road from thence to the river Isis or Thames; for building a bridge across the said river; and for making a road from thence to join the present road leading from Leachlade to Inglesham; and for repairing, widening, turning and altering the said last mentioned road to and through the town of Highworth, in the county of Wilts, to the present turnpike road leading from Cricklade to Swindon, in the same county," will, at their next meeting, to be held, by adjournment, at the New Inn, in Leachlade, on Tuesday the 14th day of August next, at ten o'clock in the forenoon, receive proposals (sealed up) and contract for building a bridge across the said river, at the bottom of the Old Red Lion Close, in Leachlade, agreeably to one of two plans, sections, and particulars, directed to be made by Mr. Daniel Harris, of Oxford; one for building a bridge of stone, and the other of wood; plans of which will be left with him, and at the New Inn aforesaid, for inspection.

Any person or persons who shall contract for building such bridge on either of the said plans, must give security, to the satisfaction of the trustees, for the performance of his or their contract.

By order of the Trustees,
CHARLES STEPHENS, Clerk.

15 *29 August 1796*

JAMES GRAHAM,
at the George Inn, Mitcheldean,

Has great pleasure in returning his respectful Thanks for the liberal support he has received, and announces to the Public, that the new road through his Majesty's Forest of Dean, leading from Mitcheldean to Colford and Monmouth, which is the high road from Glocester to South Wales, is already greatly improved, and in a short time will be equal to any in this part of the country. It is allowed that Travellers will save a mile at least by taking this way from Glocester to Monmouth, and when accurately measured it is imagined that the saving will be found to be still greater . . .

16 *21 November 1796*

The late scarcity of Coal, owing to the deficiency of water in the Severn, is, at length amply relieved, by the arrival of a fleet of Colliers. Places at a distance, that usually were provided for their Winter consumption at an earlier period of the year, must now be supplying themselves at a season very disadvantageous to our Vale Roads, the reputation of which has long been called in question by strangers unacquainted with the heavy expence at which our materials are procured. It is, however, remarked, on the subject of our Roads, that those methods for their improvement, which may be adopted with little expence, are not so universally employed, as necessity seems to demand in a low, inclosed country, of deep soil; namely, felling trees, lowering fences, and cleansing water-courses. The instances of neglect in these points are considered as standing without excuse or apology.

17 *15 May 1797*

Glocester, May 6, 1797.

NORTHGATE PIKE.

Persons willing to supply the Trustees of this Pike with 100 Tons of Bristol or Chepstow Stone, for the use of the Turnpike Road, are desired to send their proposals for that purpose to the Bank of Messrs. Niblett, Fendall, and Co. in Glocester.

18 *2 April 1798*

TO THE PRINTER

SIR,
  I beg, through your Paper, to assure the Commissioners of the Road from Newent to Dymock, and from thence to Kempley, that if the Road be not made safe this Summer, an indictment will be preferred. I expect soon to hear some poor wretch has lost his horse in the mud. I must observe, such Roads disgrace a country.

A COMMISSIONER.

19 *29 November 1813*

Intended New Road from Cirencester to Stroud.

The principal Inhabitants of Minchinhampton, Nailsworth, Horsley, Woodchester, Avening, and the Places lying south of the present Road, and other Persons, Owners of Land through which the proposed Road is intended to pass, having taken into consideration the effects which would be produced if the said intended Road should be made, and it appearing to them that such intended Road is not only altogether unnecessary and impracticable, but would be highly injurious to the Market and Post Town of Minchinhampton, (where the Excise and other Public Business is transacted,) and the Places above-mentioned; and they are also of opinion, that the present Road being so completely central, as to be equally beneficial, as well to the Inhabitants of Stroud, Chalford, and other Places, north of the same Road, as also to all the surrounding Villages and Places, is the only proper line; and that the Hill from Stroud to Rodborough (the only objectionable part of the said Road) may be avoided at a very small expence, by turning the present Road at the Bear Inn, on Rodborough Hill, a little to the north, by which means the descent into Stroud may be rendered perfectly easy.
  Notice is hereby given, That a Subscription is already opened for the purpose of opposing the Bill in Parliament for the making the said intended Road, and all Persons willing to subscribe, are to apply at the Office of Mr. Joseph Mountain, Attorney-at-Law, Cirencester, or on Tuesdays, at his Office, in Minchinhampton aforesaid.

Stone quarries on the River Avon below Bristol in 1792. Much roadstone was supplied to Gloucestershire turnpike trusts from these quarries.

20   *1 May 1820*

Notice is hereby given, That all Persons disposed to treat for Lowering the Hill on the Turnpike Road entering the town of Newnham from Chepstow, by taking off the upper part of the same, and raising the Foot of the said Hill, securing the Walls on each side, and providing for the safe Passage of Travellers during the progress of the work, and finishing the whole in a workmanlike manner, according to a Plan and Specification thereof, deposited for inspection at the Bear Inn, Newnham, are desired to send in their Estimates for such improvement, on or before the 19th day of May next, to Messrs. Evans and Son, Solicitors, Chepstow.

21   *10 July 1820*

A number of workmen are now busily engaged in levelling the hill near the turnpike, at the entrance to the borough of Tewkesbury from this city; and we understand that the active Commissioners of that District of Roads, intend immediately to widen the Mythe Hill, near the entrance to the town from the Worcester road, and to make it much more easy of ascent.

22   *23 October 1820*

A Correspondent requests us to state, that the New Road from Stroud to Cheltenham through Painswick, being completed to Prinknash Park, was opened on the 1st of August, by the Commissioners, who afterwards sat down to a sumptuous repast at the Falcon Inn, Painswick; and on the following day, upwards of 100 of the Contractor's workmen were regaled with a dinner at the Bell Inn. The remaining part of the road was let on the 5th of Aug. to Mr. C. Kemp, to whom great credit is due for the masterly way in which the work has been already carried on, and the good conduct and orderly behaviour of his men.

23   *26 March 1821*

BLACK ROCK, on the BANK of the Avon,
At the HOTWELLS, near BRISTOL

James Poole begs to inform Surveyors of Roads, Contractors for Public Works, Builders, and Persons concerned for Sea Walls, that he is enabled to supply them with Stones adapted for the above purposes, and to any extent, such as Hewn Stones of the largest size for Masonry, in large Works, Wall Stones for Buildings, Rough Stones for Roads, Pitching Stones ready worked, for Streets, Yards, and Crossings.

   The qualities of these Stones are recommended by the most eminent Surveyors, to be of a very superior description for the above uses, and are peculiarly adapted for the Repair of Roads, as they contain bitumen, consequently are not affected by frost, and have a sufficient portion of lime to cause them to unite; they are the hardest and most durable Stones to be met with, which is manifest from the reluctance of workmen to break them, who have been accustomed to lime stone. Several districts of roads at a great distance from the quarry, and attended with considerable cost for carriage, are supplied with this stone, and proved to be much cheaper than using a softer material alone, but which may be mixed by way of alloy to great advantage; they are unrivalled also for Masonry, not only for durability but appearance; a beautiful specimen may be seen at the new Gaol of Bristol, the outward wall of which is built entirely of this stone. The Quarry is situate the first in ascending the Avon, on the left-hand side.

The Docks for Vessels to load in are safe and commodious, and seldom detained more than one tide.

A Foreman lives at the Quarry. Address (if by letter, post-paid) to J. Poole, Coal Wharf, Hotwell-Road, near Bristol.

CHAPTER TWO

Inns

Town Inns and Country Inns

The inn was the unit on which the whole system of road transport rested. Besides providing bed and board for travellers, inns were the termini or staging-posts for coach services, in which the innkeeper was often himself directly involved, either as a full partner in a firm or as a contractor engaged to 'horse' a coach over a certain stage. They also supplied facilities for 'posting', the hiring out to the private traveller of post-chaises to carry him over the next stage of his journey (nos. 34, 36). The keeper of a large inn presided over a considerable establishment of waiters, cooks, scullions, boot-blacks, hairdressers, ostlers, and chaise-drivers and was often a notable figure in the local community, to which his inn brought trade and much indirect employment; a saddler's shop in Cirencester advertised for sale in 1752 (*G.J.* 17 Oct.) was said to derive its main advantage from its position opposite the King's Head 'which is the head inn, and from whence there is business enough to employ one man.' At Gloucester the landlords of the two leading inns ranked among the wealthiest citizens. Giles Greenaway, who kept the Kings Head, bought the manor of Little Barrington in 1779, shortly after he left the inn. John Phillpotts, landlord of the Bell from 1782 to 1791, was able to educate his sons for the professions: one became a bishop and another became a barrister and M.P.

Road transport, and therefore inns, played an important role in the economy of most Gloucestershire towns during this period. Even for a town like Tewkesbury with diverse functions that included stocking-knitting and malting industries, a busy agricultural market, and a major share in the trade on the Severn, road traffic was regarded as a major support. By the 1820s more than thirty stagecoaches a day with many other vehicles were passing down its main street and bringing custom to its two large inns, the Swan and the Hop Pole, and the many smaller establishments (no. 37; Bennet, *Tewkes.* p. 203). In some of the smaller towns, where there was no particular local industry and only a very limited market trade, the roads and the inns serving them played a vital

The Bell inn, Gloucester, c. 1830. This was an important coaching and social centre, one of the two leading inns of the city.

role. The case of Lechlade is illustrated later (Chapter IV, nos. 125–9), while the diminutive market town of Mitcheldean provides another example. Mitcheldean was a focal point of traffic in the Forest of Dean area: one of the main routes from Gloucester into South Wales was crossed there by lesser routes, turnpiked in 1768, leading from the Severn passages towards Ross and Hereford. At least two of its inns, the King's Arms and the George, were in that class of coaching and posting inn that found it worthwhile to advertise regularly in the *Journal* (no. 32; Chapter I, no. 15).

A large town inn like the Swan at Tewkesbury or the George at Stroud (nos. 37–8) had other functions besides those directly related to road transport, performing some of the roles later taken over by theatres, public halls, and court-rooms. A variety of events, including balls and assemblies, entertainments by travelling showmen, meetings of organisations ranging from friendly societies to turnpike trustees, sales and auctions, the transaction of business on market days, and sessions of minor courts, might regularly take place there. Events advertised at the Bell in Gloucester in the spring of 1743 (*G.J.* 1, 29 Mar.; 17 May) included a ball, an inter-county cockfight, and a course of lectures on philosophy. Smaller town inns lacked the facilities for such functions or for playing a major role in coaching but sometimes adopted some specialised role in road transport. The extracts below show one of Gloucester's smaller inns servicing the carriers on a particular route (no. 26) and another providing accommodation for Welsh drovers and acting as a depot for the distribution of coal brought to the city by its river trade (no. 27).

Inns in the countryside or in small villages were more exclusively dependent on road travel, and advertisements for their sale or letting often listed as the first, and sometimec only, detail the route on which they stood (nos. 29–30). Some of the country innkeepers, however, found other ways to supplement their income. Advertisements below show the landlord at Perrot's Brook trading on his position near Cerney Downs (where the annual Cirencester races were run) to offer attractions to sporting gentlemen (no. 28); Richard Hall of Framilode dealing on the side in some of the commodities which the trade on the River Severn brought to his door (no. 33); and the family at the George at Wheatenhurst laying on facilities for those who favoured salt-water bathing for their health (no. 35).

Many country inns occupied isolated positions, determined by the crossing of two important roads, by the need for a staging-post on a particular coaching-route, or, in the case of the many inns sited just above or below some steep hill, by the need for a place where the teams

The High Street, Cheltenham, c. 1740, with a coach changing horses outside the Plough inn. The stepping stones enabled pedestrians to cross the central channel of the street, down which the River Chelt was periodically diverted as a means of street-cleansing.

of horses could be watered and perhaps extra horses added or unhitched. The factors which governed the siting of such inns are sometimes no longer evident, leaving them in modern times the unrelated and apparently illogical points in a pattern that has been destroyed. For example, it is no longer evident to the passing motorist that Tiltups Inn above Nailsworth on the Cheltenham–Bath road relates not to that route, which it predates by many years, but to the crossroads formed by two older roads, now partly disused; or that the position on Ermin Street at Beechpike of the inn called the Highwayman (the name is a modern but not inappropriate invention: cf. Chapter VI, no. 193) was determined by a crossroads formed there with the old Cheltenham–Tetbury road, which, before the building of a new turnpike along the Colesbourne valley, also brought travellers between Cheltenham and Cirencester up to join Ermin Street at that point.

Some of the isolated country inns date from a period well before the full development of coach or waggon traffic. Those at Perrot's Brook and Ready Token among the examples below (nos. 25, 28) were two of the links in a chain of inns ranged along the road that was once the main Gloucester to London route, described as such by Ogilby in 1675 (*Britannia*, pp. 29, 110). In the coaching era that road lost most of its traffic to the routes via Oxford and via Cirencester and Lechlade. Welsh drovers, however, continued to travel to London by this historic route (named after them 'the Welsh Way') and to bring custom to its traditional stopping-places, including the Perrot's Brook and Ready Token inns and the ancient Barnsley inn, the Greyhound, which lay between them. (The fact that the sign of the Ready Token inn is given in 1738 as the 'Ready Token Ash' may seem to support the theory that the curious place-name derives from a prominent tree which became a familiar landmark for travellers; but, the explanation of place-names being a notoriously treacherous field, some earlier and more definite evidence is needed on this point).

On some of the principal routes of the county were to be found small clusters of inns, which with a few adjoining cottages, probably including blacksmith's and wheelwright's shops, formed hamlets that were almost totally sustained by road transport. Birdlip on the Gloucester–Cirencester road, aptly described in the 1680s as 'a thoroughfare village', was one such place (Hist. MSS. Com. *13th Report II*, pp. 303–4). Another, probably once the busiest of all such roadside hamlets in the county, was Newport on the Gloucester–Bristol road (nos. 24, 39). There were at least three inns at Newport during the 18th and early 19th centuries, for it stood roughly halfway between Gloucester and Bristol and was one of the staging-points for the coaches on that route. In the early days of coaching when the journey between the two cities took the best part of a day, the system was for coaches to leave each place in the morning and meet at Newport, where after a break for a meal they would exchange their passengers and return to their starting-points (e.g. Chapter III, no. 64).

24 *4 June 1722*

Whereas by printed Advertisements, dispers'd up and down the Country, it has been industriously given out that the Widow Wiltshire having left off keeping the Crown Inn in Newport, in the Road between Gloucester and Bristol, where the Stage-Coaches did use to put up; the said Coaches do now meet and put up at the Sign of the Red Lion over against the said House: This is to certifie the Public, that the Coaches, Carriers, &c. do still continue to meet and put up at the Crown Inn aforesaid; where all Gentlemen and others may be as well entertain'd and accommodated as at any Inn on the Road whatsoever,

By me,
THOMAS PHELPS

25 *30th May 1738*

This is to give Notice,

That Thomas Skillin, who kept Barnsly-Inn for these Thirteen Years last past, is remov'd from thence to his own House, the Sign of the Ready-Token Ash, at Ready-Token, lying between Fairford and Barret's-Brook, in the same Road to London as his former House; and between Burford and Cirencester, in the Oxford Road to Bath: It's a new-built House, with good Stabling, and is pleasantly situated, with a fine Prospect: Where all Gentlemen, Ladies, &c. may depend upon meeting with good Entertainment, and the most reasonable and civil Usage, from their Humble Servants,

Thomas and Susanna Skillin

N.B. At the same Place may be had good Wines, good October Beer, and good Herefordshire Cyder.

26 *16 October 1739*

This is to give Notice,

That George Cowles, is remov'd from the Red-Lion in the Lower North-Gate-street, Gloucester, to the Lamb in the same Street; where the Hereford and Monmouth Carriers put up every Week.

27 *10 January 1744*

Notice is hereby given,

That the Inn, called the Black Spread-Eagle, in the Lower Northgate-Street,

Gloucester, is now kept by Thomas and Sarah Cole, where all Gentlemen and Others may depend on civil Usage and good Entertainment.

N.B. There is Stabling for above an hundred Horses, and a large Yard stock'd with Coal for the Use of the Hill-Country Waggons, and a Parcel of very fine Hay in the Stables; and at Lady-Day next there will be fine Grazing Grounds for Depasturing Welch Cattle in their Way to London.

28 *18 September 1750*

This is to give Notice,

That the House, known by the Sign of the Huntsman and Hounds, formerly the New-Inn, at Berrot's Brook, on the Road between Gloucester and Fairford, is now kept by William Ody, Servant to the late Earl of Pembroke, and compleatly fitted up and accommodated for the Entertainment of Gentlemen and Travellers; the Favour of whose Company he humbly hopes for, as it shall be his utmost Endeavour to merit it.

There is a Dog-Kennel neatly compleated, and a Pack of Hounds kept, to pleasure any Gentlemen that like the Diversion of Hunting.

N.B. At the said House will be given a good Hunting-Saddle, of Two Guineas Value, to be Run for, the Tuesday after Michaelmas Day, by any Horse, Mare, or Gelding that never won 10l. at any one Time; a Whip for the 2d Horse, and a Pair of Spurs for the 3d Horse: To start exactly at One o'Clock.

29 *22 November 1762*

To be Lett at Lady-Day next,

The White-Hart Inn in Colford, in the Forest of Dean, in the County of Gloucester, situate on the great Roads from London to South-Wales, and from Bristol to Hereford . . .

30 *3 January 1763*

To be Lett at Lady-Day next,

The Inn, called the Red-Lion, mostly new-built, situate at Falfield, in the Parish of Thornbury, in the County of Glocester, and adjoining to the Turnpike Road leading from Bristol to Glocester . . .

31 *23 May 1763*

To be Lett,
And entered upon at Michaelmas, or any
Time sooner,

The CROWN INN, now kept by Josias Cooke, opposite the Corn Market-

House, in Cheltenham. It is a Farmer's Inn, and used by most of the Dealers, and hath good Stall Stabling and Room for an hundred Horses . . .

32 *3 December 1764*

Joseph Tibbs, of the King's-Arms Inn, in Michel-Dean in the County of Glocester, Brother to John Tibbs, at the Beaufort-Arms Inn, in Monmouth, begs Leave to acquaint the Publick, That he has now finished another Stall Stable for twenty Horses, and has lately bought four very good Chaise Horses, and some Saddle Horses. Such Noblemen, Gentlemen, Travellers, and others, who will be so kind as to honour him with their Favours, may depend on the best Accomodations and most civil treatment from,

Their most obedient humble Servant,
JOSEPH TIBBS.

N.B. A new neat Post-chaise, or Charriot, may be had on the shortest Notice. This Inn lies in the pleasantest Part of the Town, and in the Road leading to Glocester, Monmouth, London, Bath, and Bristol.

Advertisement for the Ram inn, Cirencester. It dates from about 1830 but incorporates the advertisement of an earlier landlord with an engraving by Hogarth.

33 *23 April 1770*

Richard Hall, Steward to the Right Hon. Lord Ducie, having taken the House and Business of his Mother-in-Law Mrs. Mary Cullis, the NEW-INN in Framiload, solicits a Continuance of the Favours of her Friends and Customers . . .

N.B. He sells Salt, Tenby Coals, Shropshire Coals, and Stourbrige Bricks, on the most Reasonable Terms, and has a fresh Cargo of real Tenby Coals now discharging.

34 *18 August 1777*

White Lion Inn, Tetbury, Glocestershire.

Whereas several ill-disposed Persons have industriously propogated a Report in order to injure me, James Savage, of the above Inn, that I keep but one Chaise and one Pair of bad Horses: This is therefore to give Notice to the Public in general, and my Friends in particular, that I have for four Years last past kept, and still continue to keep, two neat Chaises with eight able Horses, and careful Drivers. And I return my most grateful Acknowledgments to the Nobility, Ladies, Gentlemen, Tradesmen, and others, for the many Favours already received, and hope for a Continuance of the same, and they may depend upon the best Accomodations of every Kind, and the most civil Treatment, from

Their most humble and obedient Servant,
JAMES SAVAGE.

35 *28 June 1784*

GEORGE INN, WHEATENHURST, seven miles from
GLOCESTER

Whereas it hath been reported that Elizabeth Lewis, widow of Richard Lewis, deceased, was going to decline business and leave the said Inn; This is therefore to give notice, that she has laid in a fresh stock of liquors of all kinds, and therefore humbly hopes the friends and customers of her late husband will continue their favours as she will make it her study to accomodate them, as her family has usually done for 30 years past, which will greatly oblige

Their most devoted servant,
ELIZABETH LEWIS,

N.B. She begs leave to acquaint the public in general that she continues dipping man and beast as usual in the salt-water, at that well-known convenient house on the spot, with proper dresses, by persons who have been used to dip for the family for these 30 years past.

36 *8 August 1803*

Reduced Price of Posting.

The Nobility, Gentry, and Public are respectfully informed, that they may be forwarded with neat Chaises, good Horses, and careful Drivers, at ONE SHILLING per MILE, from the following houses, viz. the Roebuck, Oxford; the Red Lion, Burford; the Lamb, Northleach; at Kilkenny; and at the Boothall, Glocester. The Landlords of these Houses take this opportunity of thanking their friends for their past favours; and they may be assured nothing shall be wanting in their power to merit a continuance of them.

THOMAS ANDREWS.

Burford, Aug. 5, 1803.

37 *4 May 1807*

CAPITAL INN,
TEWKESBURY, GLOCESTERSHIRE.
TO BE SOLD BY AUCTION, By WM. MOORE,

At the Swan Inn, Tewkesbury, on Wednesday, the 20th day of May, 1807, between the hours of Four and Six in the Afternoon, subject to such Conditions as shall be then and there produced;–

All that the said Capital and Well-accustomed Inn and Tavern, called THE SWAN, situate in a centrical part of the town of Tewkesbury aforesaid; comprising a variety of Parlours, Dining-rooms, and Bed-chambers, with large and commodious Kitchens, Cellars, Sculleries, Brew-houses, and other Offices; a Yard, with ranges of roomy and convenient Stables and Coach-houses, and every other requisite for an Inn of the first consequence, and which, for many years past, has been highly celebrated for its Posting business, as well as for its extensive regular Market-custom.

Also, All that other Well-accustomed Inn, adjoining the above, called the WHITE HART; consisting of roomy Parlours and Kitchen, large Cellars, Brewhouse, and Offices, with good and useful Stabling, and every other convenience.

All the above Premises are Freehold, and in the occupation of Mr. John Ridler, and his Under-tenant, and have the peculiar advantage, from adjoining each other, of being thrown into one, or of remaining in their present state, as may best accomodate a purchaser.

Tewkesbury is a large and populous town, situated on the Great Road from Holyhead, Liverpool, Birmingham, and Worcester, to Gloucester, Cheltenham, Bath, Bristol, and the West of England; and being surrounded with good roads, having an excellent market, and lying midway between the fashionable Watering Places of Cheltenham and Malvern, is one of the most eligible situations in the kingdom for an Inn of the first rank.

Further particulars may be known, on application to Mr. Samuel Barnes; or to Messrs. Trueman and Smith, Solicitors, in Tewkesbury. April, 1807.

38 *8 June 1812*

STROUD (FREEHOLD)
THE GEORGE
A Capital Inn for more than a Century.

To be disposed of by Private Contract, consisting of a good Assembly Room, (the only one in the Town), Dining-Parlours, several Lodging-Rooms, Out-Offices for Carriages, Granary, Stabling for 30 or more Horses, a spacious Yard, and a good Garden . . .

39 *5 August 1816*

WHITE-HART INN,
NEWPORT, GLOUCESTERSHIRE.

To be Leased for Three Lives, – All that capital, spacious, and well-accustomed House, together with the Outhouses, Stables, Yard, Garden, and Orchard thereunto belonging and adjoining, commonly called or known by the name of the WHITE HART INN, situated in the much frequented village of Newport, and now in the occupation of Mr. James Lane, Tenant at will.

The above Premises are admirably adapted for carrying on the Posting Business, as Newport is one of the greatest thoroughfares in the kingdom . . .

40 *14 January 1822*

GLOUCESTERSHIRE.
DESIRABLE INN.

To be Let by Tender, and entered upon at Lady-Day next, That old-established and well-known Inn, the Cock, at Blakeney, in this county. The South Wales Coach changes horses at this Inn every day . . .

Rival Inns (1): Andoversford versus Frogmill

The dependence of country innkeepers on road transport was most obviously demonstrated when a rival route threatened to reduce the volume of traffic passing their doors. Such rivalries as those revealed in this section and the next were not uncommon, particularly in the late 18th and the early 19th centuries when major road improvements and the building of completely new roads caused considerable alterations in some of the main routes.

Cirencester market place c. 1804. On the left of the picture a carrier's wagon waits outside the King's Head inn.

The exchange printed below concerns two inns, at Andoversford and at Frogmill, which stood on two possible roads which traffic on the busy Gloucester–Oxford–London route could use after passing Seven Springs. This was the route on which the rival coachmasters John Turner and Thomas Pruen mentioned in a later section (Chapter VI, no. 198) were operating, and an advertisement by Pruen in 1774 (*G.J.* 18 April) shows that he used the Andoversford inn as a collecting-point for his Cheltenham passengers, who were brought up there by chaise. The competition between the two inns was evidently still in progress in 1780 (*G.J.* 3 Jan) when Daniel Field, landlord at Frogmill, placed an advertisement which claimed that 'Andoversford is now entirely shut up.'

41 *29 August 1763*

John Collier, of Andoversford, in the County of Glocester, begs Leave to inform the Publick, that he has, at a considerable Expence, made great Additions to his House, and neatly and genteely fitted up the same for the Reception of Company, and to assure them, that the Road leading from Glocester to Burford and Oxford by his House, is equally as near upon an Admeasurement as the Road by Frogmill; and notwithstanding the many and repeated invidious Attempts, which have been made by an interested Neighbour to injure the said John Collier, by obliterating the Directions on the Cross-and-Hands pointing out the Road to Burford, &c. by Andoversford, yet he hopes his Accomodations and Behaviour to those who shall be pleased to honour him with their Company, will give entire Satisfaction, and totally frustrate the malevolent Designs of his Opponent.
JOHN COLLIER.

Neat Post-Chaises, with able Horses, and careful Drivers, may at all times be depended upon.

42 *5 September 1763*

Whereas an Advertisment has appeared in the Glocester and Oxford Papers, wherein . . . (*citing the above*) . . . Now as the sole Intent of the above Advertisment is calculated with the View to impose on the Publick, and to reflect upon and prejudice Thomas Humphreys, of Frogmill aforesaid, Innkeeper; he therefore begs Leave to undeceive them in this Particular, and to acquaint his Friends and Customers, That the Road from Glocester, by Frogmill, to Burford and Oxford, has, from Time immemorial, been an accustomed publick road, and the Road mentioned in the said Advertisement, by Andoversford, leads to Stow and Campden, and is not a direct Road to Burford, being Half a Mile about, and Part of it only a private Way from one Parish to another, upon Sufferance, at and for the conveniency of the Farmers. Mr. Humphreys also hereby solemnly declares, That he never, directly or indirectly, obliterated, or caused to be obliterated, any Directions put up by the said John Collier, as is most maliciously and falsely suggested by the said Advertisement; but, however such Directions were set up, yet it was done with a Design to mislead Strangers out of the main Road, and thereby draw them to his the said John Collier's House at Andoversford; so that Travellers proceeding this Way must, in order to oblige Mr. John Collier, not only go half a Mile about, but also run the Hazard of taking the Stow or Campden Road, instead of the Burford Road, before they can get into the Turnpike Road again. Mr. Humphreys has lately made several additional improvements and Alterations at Frogmill, and has provided neat Post-Chaises and able Horses; and therefore humbly hopes for the Continuance of the Favours of his Friends and Customers, as he always did, and always will do, his utmost Endeavours to oblige them in every Particular.

THO. HUMPHREYS.

Frogmill,
September 3.

Rival Inns (2): Rodborough versus Frocester

The rivalry exhibited in the following extracts was one that resulted from the creation of an entirely new turnpike route. The rivalry involved most nearly the innkeepers of the Fleece at Rodborough and the George at Frocester but others with financial stakes in the two routes concerned were also participants. Much of the story behind the rivalry will be evident from the extracts but a brief summary of the story will make them more easily followed.

The original coaching route from Gloucester to Bath left the Bristol road (the present A38) at Claypits, ran through Eastington parish (where it gave its name to the small hamlet called Bath Street), Frocester, and Nympsfield, and joined the present A46 just east of Lasborough. A notorious obstacle on that route was Frocester hill, referred to by Celia Fiennes in 1698 as 'a very steep narrow and stony hill . . . all bad way' (*Journeys*, ed. C. Morris, 1947, p. 236). It was one of the main factors that encouraged the establishment of a new Gloucester–Bath route by the building of a new road along the Nailsworth valley from Dudbridge to Tiltups End. The Nailsworth valley road was built under an Act of 1780 by a group of gentry and clothiers of the Woodchester and Nailsworth area under the leadership of that energetic reformer Sir George Onesiphorus Paul, who lived at Hill House, Rodborough, overlooking the new road. To provide staging facilities on the new road, in place of the George Inn at

Frocester which had served that purpose on the old road, a new inn called the Fleece was built. It stood just below Hill House and it was Sir George Paul who provided the site and the capital for building it (£1,369, as his personal accounts record: Glos. R.O., D 589, Paul family papers), but it appears that some of his collaborators in the new road took shares in the inn.

The immediate reaction of those interested in the old route can be seen below, but they also took the more concrete step of building a new piece of road on their route to provide an easier ascent up Frocester hill; the old road running up through the woods to the east of it can still be walked and its steepness appreciated. Nevertheless most of the traffic evidently switched to the Nailsworth valley route, in spite of advertisements extolling the beauties and advantages of the Frocester route that successive landlords of the George continued to place in the *Journal* until at least 1804 (30 Jan.). The Fleece, meanwhile, prospered, particularly after 1801 when a new road built down the Slad valley through Stroud to Lightpill put the inn on the main Cheltenham–Bath route and in receipt of some of the most fashionable custom in the land. The reputation of the Fleece was such that after it closed with the arrival of the railway age two other inns on the same road, at Lightpill and at Rooksmoor (now the Old Fleece), adopted its sign (*V.C.H. Glos.* xi. 221). The George at Frocester survived its old rival and remains open today under its new sign of the Royal Gloucestershire Hussar.

43 *18 February 1782*

ROAD from BATH to GLOCESTER.

The Trustees acting under an Act of Parliament intended to facilitate the Communication between Bath and Glocester, hereby give Notice to the Public in general, and to Travellers from the West to the North of England in particular, that the said Road is now opened, leading from near the 20 Mile Stone on the Road from Bath to Frocester Hill, through or near Nailsworth and Woodchester, to a Junction with different Glocester Roads at Cainscross. The Inconvenience of Hills so objectionable to the other Roads, will be found in this to be entirely removed without the least Increase of Distance.

With Intent to render the public Accomodation complete, a Society of Gentlemen are erecting a spacious and commodious House, situate near Woodchester, at a convenient Distance for Change of Horses between Petty-France or Cross-Hands Inn and Glocester, which will be ready to open at Michaelmas-Day next, with every Accomodation as an Inn, Tavern, and Post-House, and will consist of four large and elegant

A wagon being loaded outside the Swan inn, Tewkesbury.

Parlours, with Bar, Tap-Room, Kitchen, and all other useful Offices on the Ground Floor; 18 good Bedchambers; Cellars for 500 Hogsheads of Beer; and arched Vault for Wine, and Coach-Houses and Stables for any Number of Horses.

The said Inn to be let. Enquire at the Cross-Hands, Petty-France, or the Bell, at Glocester, where Directions for further Particulars may be obtained. No Person need apply who cannot bring a sufficient Capital to furnish the House in the handsomest Manner, and has not an established Character for Civility, and other necessary Requisites to give Credit to an Inn.

44 *6 January 1783*

To the Nobility, Gentry, &c, travelling through
Glocester to Bath

The following comparative View of the Roads are humbly submitted to their Consideration: And first, what is called the New Road from Glocester to Bath, which begins at a Place called Dudbridge, eleven Miles from Glocester: The nearest Way to get to it is, from Glocester through Standish and Stonehouse, a Cross-Country Road, with several Gates to open, in most Part of which there is not Room for two Carriages to pass each other. There is another Way to get to this Road, through Painswick, which is nothing but Hills and Vallies every Mile of it, and considerably further than the Cross-Country Road. The Advocates for the new Road say there is no Hill that Way, forgetting that it is one continued Rise from Nailsworth to a Place called Tiltups Inn, (a little Public-House) which is two Miles, that a carriage cannot be taken up faster than Horses can walk. They next say, it is nearer this Way, than the Road through Frocester, to Bath; but in this they are much mistaken, for through Frocester is almost two Miles nearer (both Roads having been actually measured by the Surveyor, whose Name is to this Advertisment.) The Accommodations on the Frocester Road are well known, the Hill very short, to get up which as quick as possible, an additional Pair of Horses is put to every Carriage going from Frocester Inn, without any further Expence to the Traveller. If a fine Country, diversified with the most beautiful Prospects, is a Recommendation, the Road through Frocester is superior to any other Road from Glocester to Bath.

Measured the two Roads above-mentioned
the 9th Day of September, 1782.

R. HALL, Land-Surveyor.

45 *13 January 1783*

The Gentlemen Subscribers to the New Branch of Road from Bath to Glocester, observe in the last Glocester Journal, an Advertisment, signed R. Hall, who, calling himself *Land* Surveyor, presumes with the most confident Assurance, to direct the Nobility, Gentry, &c. in the Choice of their Road and Accomodation, and grossly mistates Facts with evident

37

Design to attack the Property of a Gentleman who has sunk a very considerable Sum for the public Convenience.

The said Advertiser is below their Attention – but as it must be presumed he is but the Hireling of Persons, who, being dependant on public Favour, dare not insult the public Credulity in their own Name – to them, and to the Public, the Subscribers observe, that the jealous Apprehensions, implied by such Advertisements, are the most unequivocal Proofs, that their Endeavours to ornament the Country promise an Encouragement alarming to their envious Opponents.

The circumstance of so many Gentlemen consenting to expend near 7000l. on the present Improvement, speaks most decidedly their Opinion of the general Utility, and of the Efficacy to the particular Purpose of improving the Road from Bath to Glocester; if that End is answered, it matters not to the Public, whether it be by the *direct* Exertion on the Dudbridge District, or by a *consequent* one on the Frocester.

A very singular Phenomenon is indeed observable: On making the Road from Dudbridge to Tiltup's Inn, Frocester Hill (Hitherto tedious and almost perpendicular) becomes at once a Plain, the Road from Glocester to Bath shortened Two Miles, and became furnished *with Inns of the best Accomodation*: Such magic Influence might indeed be doubted, but that it is assured by such a *respectable* and *disinterested* Advertiser.

The Subscribers decline entering into invidious Comparisons on the Excellence of the two Roads, much less would they dictate to the Traveller what Road he should take. Curiosity will lead every Man to compare for himself, and his Conviction on the Fact will afterwards direct him. They only assure the Public that the road is in good Repair, and will be kept so, and that the Inn, built by Sir G. Paul, will be opened before Lady Day, with Post Horses, and every Accomodation. When, according to the said R. Hall's Distance from Glocester to Dudbridge, the Traveller can pay but 39 miles from Bath to Glocester, whereas it is well known that the usual Charge on the other Road is 41 miles.

Signed by Order of the Subscribers to the Dudbridge Road.

JAMES DALBY, Clerk to the Meetings.

46 *9 June 1783*

RODBOROUGH, GLOCESTERSHIRE
The New Road from Glocester to Bath.

Whereas the Trustees appointed to carry into Execution an Act of Parliament for making certain New Roads (intended to facilitate the Communication between Bath and Glocester, by avoiding Frocester-Hill) did some Time past give Notice, That the principal Line was compleated, and open for the Accommodation of the Public; but it appearing that the said Road was very deficient to the Purposes of the Traveller, for Want of an Inn and Post House at a convenient Distance for Change of Horses from

Glocester, a Society of Gentlemen undertook, at great Expence, further to accomodate the Public, by building an Inn on an elegant and extensive Plan.

The Subscribers to the above Undertaking hereby inform all Persons travelling from Hollyhead, and the great Northern Road through Glocester to Bath, That the Building is now finished, and opened with every Accomodation as an Inn and Post-House, at Rodborough, about 12 Miles from Glocester; by which Means they flatter themselves the Traveller will find, that the intended communication is rendered compleat.

RODBOROUGH, GLOCESTERSHIRE.

The Fleece Inn and Tavern, built at great Expence as a Center House on the new Road between Petty-France or Cross-Hands and Glocester, being now furnished with every elegant Accomodation, JAMES ELDERTON (from the George at Trowbridge) respectfully informs the Nobility and Gentry, travelling from Holyhead and the great Northern Road through Glocester to Bath, that he has taken and furnished the said House . . .

BELL INN, GLOCESTER, April 25.

J. PHILLPOTTS most respectfully begs Leave to acquaint the Nobility, Gentry, and Public, that he has fitted up the above Inn in an elegant Manner . . .

As he is immediately connected with the Fleece Inn, at Rodborough, on the New Bath Road, he begs Leave to assure the Nobility, Gentry, &c. travelling to Bath, that no Exertion will be wanting to facilitate the Posting Business thereon, and to render every Conveyance as commodious and as expeditious as possible . . .

47 *16 February 1784*

THE NEW ROAD through FROCESTER and PETTY-FRANCE to BATH.

Christopher Coleman, at the George Inn, Frocester, ever grateful for the many and repeated Favours which he has received from the Nobility, Gentry, and public, with singular Satisfaction, acquaints them that Frocester-Hill, which heretofore occasioned Inconveniences and Delays to Travellers on Account of its Steepness, is now, by a New and Judicious Cut, which avoids the Village of Nympsfield, rendered quite easy and pleasant.

From this New Road the Traveller is entertained with one of the most extensive and delightful Prospects in the Kingdom; the Eye commanding at one View, a most beautiful and highly cultivated Vale, with the River Severn, the Malvern Hills, the romantic Mountains of South-Wales, and many other pleasing and picturesque Scenes.

Being determined to exert every Means in his Power to render the Accomodation of his House perfectly agreeable, C. Coleman humbly hopes for the future Encouragement of the Public, and begs Leave to assure them, that, upon all Occasions, he will most gratefully acknowledge their Favours.

Frocester, Feb. 12, 1784.

A very exact and accurate Admeasurement of the Roads between Glocester and Bath hath been lately made, whereby it appears, that the Road through Frocester is, at least, a Mile nearer than that through Rodborough.

48 *29 September 1794*

FLEECE-INN, RODBOROUGH.

First Stage from Glocester and Cheltenham, on the Great Road from Holyhead, &c. to Bath.

E. King, impressed with gratitude, begs to return his sincere thanks to the Nobility, Gentry, Gentlemen Travellers, and others, for the very liberal support he has experienced, and assures them, every exertion shall be made use of to deserve a continuance, by paying particular attention to every part of the business. The House has received considerable improvement; great addition has been made to the Furniture, Beds, &c. The Wines and Liquors are old, and of the best qualities; prime bottled Cyder, &c.; the much esteemed Rodborough cask and bottled Beer; together with a good Larder, and every thing requisite to render an Inn comfortable. Neat Post Chaises, with capital stables of Horses, and steady Drivers.

Ladies and Gentlemen, who wish to avoid disagreeable hills, and travel with dispatch and safety through the most beautiful part of the county of Glocester, the heart of the Cloth Manufactory, and one of the most delightful Vales in the kingdom, will find themselves highly gratified and most agreeably surprized.

N.B. No advance whatever has been made in the price of posting.

'Your Humble Servant' – An Obeisance of Innkeepers

This section presents a short selection of the many innkeepers who advertised in the *Journal* over the period, though each advertisement has been curtailed to spare the reader the very similar obsequious appeals for 'favours' made by these 'humble servants' of the public; some of the advertisements in the preceding sections of this chapter will give an idea of the general tone. The types of landlord represented here include those who were born into the trade (no. 54); those who 'rose from the ranks' of inn employees – and in this connexion it was obviously a useful recommendation to have worked at the Bell, one of Gloucester's two leading inns (nos. 53, 55, 60); and a very common category, former servants. The newsman James Nott, the man who distributed the *Journal* to Hereford, is perhaps a rather unusual representative of those innkeepers who followed other trades at the same time. Such people as masons, carpenters, and blacksmiths commonly kept inns in country districts, though usually inns of the type that did only a very local trade and so were not often advertised in the newspaper.

Innkeepers of the high coaching era appear to have been a very mobile class, periodically changing houses in the course of their careers; some individuals turn up regularly in the *Journal* advertisements at different points on the network of main roads. Often the move a man made was down the same line of road, to an inn with which he would often already have business connexions. To take some Gloucester city examples in the 1790s: E. King mentioned above at the Rodborough Fleece (no. 48) had moved there from the Swan at Gloucester (*G.J.* 20 Jan. 1794); two innkeepers who came respectively to the King's Head and the Bell were both former landlords of the Castle at Benson in Oxfordshire on one of the routes from Gloucester to London (*G.J.* 17 May 1790; 30 Sept. 1793); and a later landlord of the Bell came from the Swan at Ross on one of the routes into Wales (*G.J.* 29 May 1797).

49 *7 May 1734*

Notice is hereby given,

That Samuel Harris, formerly Clothier from Inchbrooke in the Parish of Woodchester, is newly come, and keeps the Bear-Inn at the Smith's Shop, or otherwise known by the Name of Cold-Harbour, in the Great Road between Gloucester and Bath . . .

50 *1 January 1751*

NOTICE is hereby given,

That Thomas Harvey, who serv'd seven Years' Apprenticeship to a Vintner in London, and kept the George Inn, in Cheltenham, Gloucestershire, for these nine Years last past is now removed to a New, Large, Handsome, and Commodious Inn, of his own building, opposite the Market-House, in Cheltenham aforesaid, called the Swan . . .

51 *29 January 1751*

NOTICE, is hereby given, That

James Nott, Hereford Newsman, has taken the Bull-Inn in Gloucester . . .

52 *15 May 1753*

Joseph Stratford, Late Coachman to Sir Francis Fust, Bart. is Removed, from the George in Thornbury, to the White-Swan Inn, at Whitminster, which is newly fitted up, and has a Stalled Stable belonging to it . . .

53 *16 October 1753*

This is to give Notice, That Francis Adams, late Ostler to Mr. Whitefield, at the Bell-Inn, in Gloucester, Hath taken the George-Inn, at Stow on the Wold . . .

54 *16 May 1758*

Glocester, May 1.

JOHN HEATH, Jun.

Begs Leave to acquaint his Friends, (his Father having left the King's-Head Inn) That he hath fitted up the Golden-Hart, being a very commodious Inn, in the Southgate-Street . . .

55 *26 August 1760*

Glocester, August 23.

The Grey-Hound Inn in the Eastgate-Street, in this City, lately kept by Mr. Charles Cole, is now entered on by James Evans, (formerly Servant at the Bell in this City, and late Waiter at the Rose-Tavern in Cambridge) who is now fitting it up in a neat genteel Manner . . .

56 *2 December 1760*

Henry Greening, late Servant to Samuel Blackwell, Esq; begs Leave to inform the Publick, That he has taken the Falcon-Inn, in Painswick, Glocestershire, which is deemed the largest and most commodious Inn in that Town, and is just now fitted up in a genteel Manner, the greatest Part of the Furniture being entirely new . . .

57 *23 August 1779*

GLOCESTER.

William Hill, Servant to the late Lord Bishop of Glocester, begs Leave to acquaint Gentlemen, Tradesmen, and others, that he has taken and entered upon the Black Horse in the Southgate-Street . . .

58 *26 February 1787*

FROGMILL INN,

Situated 16 miles from Burford, 14 from Glocester, and 16 from Tewkesbury.

JOHN HOWES, butler to R.P. Knight, Esq; and late butler to Sir Hungerford Hoskyns, Bart. begs leave to inform the nobility and gentry, that he has taken the above established Inn; and has enlarged the stock with the choicest wines, spirits, &c. of the very best quality . . .

59 *26 February 1787*

Badminton, Jan. 1.
CHARLES AND SARAH COUNTZE

Beg Leave to inform the public, that they have entered upon the Inn lately occupied by Mr. Stevens, at Badminton, near the magnificent seat of his Grace the Duke of Beaufort . . .

As Countze has had the honour of serving his Grace the Duke of Beaufort, and other Noblemen and Gentlemen, in the capacity of a cook, his utmost endeavours will be exerted to give satisfaction in his professional line.

60 *18 April 1808*

WHITE-HART INN, LEONARD-STANLEY.
WILLIAM MORSE

Returns his thanks to his Friends and the Public, for the favours bestowed on him during his residence at the above Inn, and informs them that he has resigned the same to Mr. Mark Fricker.

MARK FRICKER,
(Late Waiter at Mr. Yearsley's, Bell Inn, Glocester,)

Solicits the favours of his Friends, Gentlemen Travellers, and the Public, at the above Inn. He assures them that the Stock of Beer is Home-brewed, and of the best quality; that he has laid in the choicest Wines and Spirits, and that every attention shall be paid to their accomodation.

April 6, 1808.

61 *28 March 1814*

Hunter's Hall Inn, Kingscote.

William Dubberly, (late Servant to Mrs. Kingscote,) most respectfully informs the Nobility, Gentry, and Public, that he has taken and entered on the above Large and Commodious Inn . . .

CHAPTER THREE

Coaches

'Performed, if God Permit' – The Main Routes

Until the beginning of the 19th century, when county directories and town guides begin to appear, the *Journal* has no rival as a source of information for the history of coaching services in Gloucestershire. This chapter gives a selection of the advertisements placed in the paper by the coach operators, together with some other material illustrating the subject.

Most of the early coach operators were based in Gloucester city, which was unchallenged in its role as the hub of the road transport system of the county. Its position on the major route from Bristol and the south-western counties up to Birmingham and the Midlands would probably have ensured this, even without its bridges which, as the lowest on the Severn and (before the mid 1820s) the only ones on the Gloucestershire stretch of the river, gave it command of the land-route from London into South Wales. It was Gloucester operators who pioneered the coaching routes into South Wales, and, as the report of John Turner's triumphal progress in 1756 shows, were regarded almost as the harbingers of civilization to that remote and backward region (no. 66). Turner's initial venture did not in fact pay and he had to withdraw the service 18 months later (*G.J.* 30 May 1758), but he was able to establish a regular service on the Brecon route again in the 1760s, aided by a programme of road improvement put in hand by local gentry (*G.J.* 15 Apr. 1765; cf. Chapter I, no. 7). That route appears to have remained very much the preserve of the Gloucester coachmasters, right up to the day in 1854 when the Brecon mail, draped in black, made its last run, signalling to the city the final triumph of the railways (*G.J.* 1 Apr. 1854). Gloucester coaches also operated on the more southerly route via Newport and Cardiff and established connexions with the Irish packets plying from Milford Haven (no. 70).

Among the market towns of the county Cirencester probably ranked second to Gloucester as a coaching centre. Its strategic position on the main route from central Gloucestershire to London, to which it had a

made, (on its
re immediate-
ourfuit of her,
Norfolk-ftreet
lately carry'd
id committed
:tage Coaches
little beyond
1: They took
d fome filver,
uff Box; and
:hree Women,
Coach going
n North-Hall
ay-men, who
ord Bifhop of
above thirty
Coach, who

iam Tweede,
1 on the Back
er to Sale in
eld for Shop-
once admitted
for marrying
g.

d the Fortune
Lisbon.——
om South Ca-
the Charity,
le Swan, from

'S.
rmiſſion,
:-EATER,
;
or to the Court of
refent Majefty K.
it Satisfaction, as
y, in fuch a won-
ty of Human Na-
it in a Chair, with
her, and fets him
: of 4 or 5 Pound

Gloucefter, Briftol, and Bath Stage-Coaches.

SETS out from Thomas Winſton's, near
the New Pear in Gloucefter, every Wednefday and
Friday Morning at Six a-Clock, to the Lamb in Broad-Mead,
Briftol, and from thence to the White-Hart in Bath.
Likewife another Coach fets out from the Lamb in Broad-
Mead aforefaid, every Wednefday and Friday Morning, to
Gloucefter the fame Day.
Note, Thofe Paffengers that want to go from Bath to
Gloucefter, may go from the White-Hart in Bath (in a Coach
kept for that Purpofe) to the Lamb in Briftol every Tuefday
and Thurfday, and from thence to Gloucefter the next Day.
Perform'd (if God permit) by

William Simkins, Briſtol.
Thomas Winſton, Gloucefter.

☞ At both the faid Places you may be furnifh'd with a very
good Coach or Chariot: Likewife a new Herfe, very reafonable.

This is to give Notice,

That Robert Arnold of the City of Gloucefter, WAGGONER,

(having purchafed the Cuftom and Bufinefs of
Mr. John Wood, lately deceas'd)

Continues to keep the ufual and conftant Stage between this
City and London; and carries all manner of Goods, Wares,
Merchandizes, and Paffengers, at reafonable Rates; and fets
out from his own Houfe in the North-Gate-ftreet in Gloucefter, on Tuefday the firft of April, by Three in the Morning,
and goes into the King's-Head in the Old Change, on Friday
following; and fets out from thence on Saturday Morning,
about Eleven a Clock, and returns into Gloucefter the Wednefday following.
Whoever hath any Goods to be carried below Gloucefter,
(where no Stage goes through) upon an Agreement made at
his own Houfe in Gloucefter, or at his Inn in London aforefaid, the fame will be fafely deliver'd.
And as Mr. Wood formerly kept a Waggon to Ledbury,
during the Summer-feafon, the fame will, upon Incouragement, be continued.
Perform'd, if GOD permit,

An Exprefs
the King of P
and that the (
Pox at Mofco
Six Ships o
fion next Wee
On Wednef
Vittualling (
maſters of Shi
to Gibraltar.
On Thurfd
to 306,000 l.
One Tidew
others fuſpen
about threefc
brought in;
mined to difcl
the leaſt Thin
er Favour do
We hear th
the Relief of.
arreſted fhall,
Oath to their
in fuch cafe,
fhall happen t
their Charge o
finement, in a
fame Circumf
upon refufal, f
But that if it
Concealment o
purpófe to de
Debtor fhall b
therein.
Laſt Tuefd
ſtead Downs,
won the Purſ
Mr. Rice the
the 20 l. Pl
Prince was p
On Thurfc
feller, was ta
Majefty's Me
ing the Counti

South Sea

regular coach service as early as 1696 (*London Gazette*, 11–14 May, 1696), led to Cirencester's coach operators exercising a dominant role in the London services from neighbouring towns, such as Stroud, Minchinhampton, and Tetbury.

The other sizable market town of the county, Tewkesbury, was a busy staging-post on the Bristol–Midlands route but does not appear to have had direct London services in the 18th century and was probably served through Gloucester. Cheltenham also was very much a satellite of Gloucester for coaching purposes in the 18th century, being connected to the Gloucester–London services by post-chaises, running up to Frogmill or Andoversford (*G.J.* 25 Apr. 1768; 18 Apr. 1774). Cheltenham's growth by the beginning of the 19th century is reflected in the re-routing of the Gloucester–London coaches through the town, and by 1822 its coach operators were running a greater number of services than those of Gloucester (nos. 75, 80; *Pigot's Dir.* (1822–3), 50–1, 60–1). The balance of power in terms of road transport was further altered by the opening of new bridges over the Severn at the Haw and the Mythe, near Tewkesbury, in 1825 and 1826. Both Cheltenham and Tewkesbury benefited from the new routes established across the river to Hereford and Wales, and Gloucester's ancient hegemony was at last under threat; in 1827 a plan by the Post Office to move the direct Hereford and Brecon mail route away from Gloucester to the new Mythe bridge road was strongly resisted by the city corporation (*G.J.* 1, 8 Dec. 1827; Glos. R.O., GBR, B 3/14, ff.80v.–81).

A traveller in the 1820s was able to look back on a revolution in road transport which had occurred over a period of some fifty years. To him the coach advertisements of the first half of the 18th century – when journeys were 'performed, if God permit' and the time taken from Gloucester to London was three days in winter and two in summer – were as much a curiosity as they are to us (nos. 62–3). The gradual improvement of the roads and advances in coach design enabled operators on the Gloucester–London route to advertise a time of 'one day' (actually a long and tiring 21 hours) by 1765 and of 14 hours by 1822 (nos. 68, 80). Coaches in their 'golden age' provided a fast, efficient network of communications, their speed, if not always their safety, guaranteed by the number on the road and the intense rivalry between the different operators (nos. 72, 76, 78). John Spencer's Booth Hall coach office (no. 80) was one of five in Gloucester from which services were run in the 1820s, when nearly 100 coaches a day passed through the city (Counsel, *Gloucester*, pp. 209, 242–34).

As journeys began to offer some prospect of enjoyment and not just prolonged discomfort, coach-driving became a craze of the wealthy fraternity, whose younger members delighted to take the reins of the crack public coaches or, like Roynon Jones (no. 74), engage in contests with their own vehicles. Another enthusiast for coach-driving who possibly played a part in the 'matches against time' referred to in 1802 was Charles Apperley, later widely known as 'Nimrod' the sporting journalist. Apperley was then living locally, at Wotton near Gloucester, and he later recalled how he saved Roynon Jones from being cheated out of a large sum in a Cheltenham gambling den which they frequented (Nimrod, *My Life and Times*, ed. E.D. Cuming, 1927, pp. 244–5).

The character of the men who drove the coaches, shown in an unfavourable light in two extracts in this chapter (nos. 77, 84), appears to have been adversely affected by the patronage of the sporting aristocracy and gentry, though a natural pride in their skill at the difficult business of four-in-hand driving was also a cause of their conceited and overbearing manner. George Borrow, in *The Romany Rye* (Chapter 26), wrote: 'The stage-coachmen of England, at the time of which I am speaking (i.e. 1825), considered themselves mighty fine gentry, nay, I verily believe the most important personages of the realm, and their entertaining this high opinion of themselves can scarcely be wondered at; they were low fellows, but masters at driving; driving was in fashion, and sprigs of nobility used to dress as coachmen and imitate the slang and behaviour of coachmen, from whom occasionally they would take lessons in driving as they sat beside them on the box, which post of honour any sprig of nobility who happened to take a place on a coach claimed as his unquestionable right; and then these sprigs would smoke cigars and drink sherry with the coachmen in bar-rooms, and on the road; and, when bidding them farewell, would give them a guinea or half-guinea, and shake them by the hand, so that these fellows, being low fellows, very naturally thought no small liquor of themselves, but would talk familiarly of their friends lords so and so, the honourable misters so and so, and Sir Harry and Sir Charles, and be wonderfully saucy to any one who was not a lord, or something of the kind; . . . for as the insolence of these knights was vast, so was their rapacity enormous; they had been so long accustomed to have crowns and half-crowns rained upon them by their admirers and flatterers, that they would look at a shilling, for which many an honest labourer was happy to toil for ten hours under a broiling sun, with the utmost contempt . . .' The coachman's fraud mentioned in no. 77 was evidently a common one: 'Nimrod' (op. cit. pp. 242–3) refers to it as 'swallowing' a passenger'.

62   *11 June 1722*

This is to give notice that the London and Oxford Flying Coach will come to the King's Head in Ross every Wednesday before Dinner, and returns from thence every Thursday at one of the clock, for Gloucester; from whence it goes to Oxford on Friday, and reaches London on Saturday. Price to Oxford 17s. to London 1l. 7s.,

Perform'd (if God permit) by
William Haynes, of Oxford.

Note, Places may be taken at the King's Head in Ross aforesaid, at the New Inn in Oxford, the White Horse in Fleet-street, or at Mr. John Harris's, Mercer, in Gloucester.

63 *23 March 1731*

Gloucester, Oxon, and London Stage-Coach began Flying on Monday the 15th of this Instant March, and will continue to go in two Days three times a Week all the Summer. Places are to be taken of John Harris, Mercer in Gloucester, where any Person may be furnish'd with By-Coaches, Chariot, Chaise, a Mourning Coach and new Hearse, with able Horses, to any Part of Great-Britain, at reasonable Rates.

Coach traffic in Tewkesbury High Street (looking south to the Cross), *c.* 1830.

5 October 1731

Notice is hereby given,

That the Gloucester Stage-Coach to London, leaves off Flying on Saturday next the 9th of this Inst. and goes to London in three Days as usual, on Mondays and Thursdays . . .

JOHN HARRIS.

64 *8 April 1735*

The Old GLOUCESTER and BRISTOL
STAGE-COACHES,
(In one Day.)

Set out, as usual, from the Golden-Heart in Gloucester, and from the Lamb in Broad-Mead, Bristol, and meet and dine at the Red-Lyon in Newport. The Stage begins on Wednesday the 16th Instant, and will continue every Wednesday and Friday, during the Summer Season. Each Passenger allow'd to carry Fourteen Pounds Weight, and to pay for all above.

Perform'd (if God permit) by
THOMAS HOW, at the Golden-Heart
in Gloucester, and
JAMES WIMBLE, at the Lamb
in Broad-Mead, Bristol.

65 *15 March 1743*

Cirencester FLYING STAGE-COACH
(In One Day.)
Begins on Monday the 21st of March Instant.

Goes from the King's-Head-Inn in Cirencester, every Monday, Wednesday and Friday, to the Bell-Savage Inn on Ludgate-Hill, London; and returns every Tuesday, Thursday, and Saturday, at the usual Hours.

Perform'd (if GOD permit) by
{ JAMES KEMP,
and
EDWARD BIGGS.

66 *9 November 1756*

Extract of a Letter from Abergavenny, Monmouthshire, Nov. 6.

"Mr. Turner's Scheme, of setting up a Weekly Stage between London and Brecon, is so highly approved, that last Saturday, on his Arrival here, he was welcomed with the ringing of Bells, and the greatest Marks of the Approbation of the whole Country. Several Gentlemen of the Neighbourhood met Mr. Turner, at the Angel Inn, and entered into a voluntary Subscription for repairing the Roads, that no Impediment of that Sort might hinder him from prosecuting so useful an Undertaking. The same Encouragement has been given him at Brecon, and at all the Towns through which the Stage passes."

67 *1 April 1765*

BRISTOL AND BIRMINGHAM
STAGE COACH,
In One Day and a Half,

Began on Tuesday March 19; sets out from the Lamb in Broad-Mead, Bristol, every Tuesday and Thursday, at four o'Clock in the Morning, lies at the Hop-Pole in Worcester that Night, and gets into Birmingham by 12 o'Clock the next Day; returns from the Dolphin Inn in Birmingham every Tuesday and Thursday, at four o'Clock in the Morning, lies at Glocester that Night, and gets to Bristol by 12 o'clock the next Day. Each Passenger to pay 18s. and to be allowed 14 lb. Weight Luggage, all above to pay 1d. per Pound. Children in Lap and Outside Passenger to pay Half Price, and have no Luggage allowed.

THO. WILTS, Bristol,
JOHN TURNER, Glocester,
THO. GARMSTON, Worcester.

68 *15 April 1765*

The Glocester Double Post-Coach,
In ONE DAY,

Will begin on Sunday Night the 28th Inst and will continue to set out every Night in the Week, Saturdays excepted, at ten o'Clock, from the Coach-Office in Glocester, and from the Bolt-and-Tun Inn in Fleet-street, London, and will arrive in Glocester and London at seven o'Clock the next Evening.

The Proprietors' Motive for introducing the Double Post-Coach is to remedy the Inconvenience of a middle Passenger's Situation in the common Stages. This Carriage is divided into two distinct Apartments, each to contain four Passengers. Upon this Plan every one of the Company will be accomodated with a Seat as agreeable and airy as in any modern Vehicle.

The Post-Coach is fitted up in an elegant Manner, and hung upon Steel Springs constructed to render its Motion as easy as that of the lightest Post-Chaise.

By Means of this double Coach we are enabled to continue the Price as usual at 1l. 3s.; and for Outside Passengers and Children in Lap half Price.

Parcels will be delivered with the greatest Care; but we will not be answerable for Things of Value unless entered as such. Allowance to each Inside Passenger 14 lb.

Performed by
WILLIAM and JOHN TURNER.

69 *15 April 1782*

COACHES.

The Proprietors of the different Stage-Coaches on the North Road finding themselves materially injured by the present Price paid by Passengers

50

between Bristol and Glocester, as being inadequate to the Expences of Duty, &c. attending the said Coaches, beg Leave to acquaint the public, that they are necessitated for the future to charge Eight Shillings for each Inside Passenger, and Four Shillings Outside, from Bristol to Glocester, and in Proportion any Part of the Road.

J. WEEKS,			G. HINKS,		
T. JANE,	}	Bristol	T. JONES,	}	Glocester
G. POSTON,			J. PAIN,		

70 *29 August 1785*

Glocester, August 14, 1785.
BELL INN,
JOHN PHILLPOTTS, and Co.
PROPRIETORS OF THE ORIGINAL
London and Glocester Post-Coaches,

Beg leave to acquaint the Public, that they continue to run at the usual Hour and Price, and flatter themselves that their accustomed punctuality will insure them a continuance of that favour and patronage which they have hitherto so amply experienced, and that no endeavours of theirs may be wanting to render the communication to the South-West part of Ireland, as compleat and expeditious as possible, the following Coaches and Packets are this day established:

For MILFORD HAVEN, CORK, WATERFORD, and
all the South-West part of IRELAND.
An elegant Post-Coach,
(Carrying four persons only, inside)

Will set out from the Angel-Inn behind St. Clement's Church, in the Strand, every Sunday and Tuesday, at two o'clock in the afternoon, and arrive at Hubberstone, on Milford Haven, every Wednesday and Friday at the same hour. Returns from thence every Tuesday and Thursday at twelve at noon, and arrives in London every Friday and Sunday morning.

The above Coach goes through Oxford, Glocester, Chepstow, Newport, Cardiff, and the Delightful Vale of Glamorgan, to Swansea, Carmarthen, Haverfordwest, and Hubberstone; where three good well-manned Packets are constantly plying, to convey Passengers and Parcels to and from Waterford.

Carriage and passage from London to Waterford 5*l*. 5s.; ditto Hubberston 4*l*. 4s.; ditto Carmarthen 3*l*. 12s.; ditto Swansea 3*l*.; ditto Cardiff 2*l*. 10s.; ditto Chepstow 1*l*. 17s.; ditto from Hubberston to Carmarthen 13s.; ditto to Swansea 1*l*. 4s.; ditto to Cardiff 2*l*. 2s.; ditto to Chepstow 2*l*. 12s. 6d.; ditto to Glocester 3*l*.; ditto to London 4*l*. 4s. The passengers sleep at the Angel Inn, Cardiff, and at the Ivy Bush Inn, Carmarthen, going down and coming up. They also stop at the Bell Inn, Glocester, and the Angel Inn, Oxford.

Outside passengers, and children in lap, to pay half price . . .

51

ROYAL HOTEL COACH OFFICE,
Cheltenham.

IMPROVED SAFETY & ELEGANT LIGHT POST COACHES,
DAILY TO THE FOLLOWING PLACES.

LONDON The Magnet Safety Coach, every Morning at ½ past Six o'clock thro' Northleach, Burford, Witney, Oxford, Henley, Maidenhead, Slough & Hounslow.

LONDON Royal Veteran, every Morning at ½ past Eight thro' Northleach, Burford, Witney, Oxford, Wycomb & Uxbridge.

OXFORD & LONDON Two Day Coach every day except Sundays at Twelve o'clock Sleeps at Oxford.

OXFORD Coaches, every Morning at ½ past Six & ½ past Eight o'clock.

BATH The Original Post Coach, every day except Sundays at Nine o'clock through Gloucester & Rodborough.

BATH The York House Coach, every day except Sundays at Two o'clock through Painswick & Stroud.

BRISTOL The Traveller, every day except Sundays at Twelve o'clock thro' Gloucester & Newport.

BRISTOL The Royal Pilot, through Gloucester every Monday, Wednesday, & Friday, at ½ past One o'clock.

EXETER The Traveller, every day except Sundays, at Twelve o'clock thro' Gloucester, Bristol, Bridgewater, Taunton, Wellington, Collumpton & Exeter, where it meets Coaches for Plymouth.

GLOUCESTER Accommodation Coaches every Morning at Nine, ½ past Nine & Twelve, o'clock, Afternoon at ½ past One, Three, Five & Seven o'clock, in the Evening.

TEWKESBURY Coaches every Morning except Sundays, at Eight & Twelve, Afternoon at ½ past One, every Evening at 8.

MALVERN The Mercury, every Morning at ½ before Eight, except Sundays, to Essington's Hotel, Malvern Wells, arrives at Eleven o'clock, leaves Malvern at Five.

LIVERPOOL The Magnet, every Tuesday, Thursday & Saturday, at Twelve o'clock, thro' Worcester, Birmingham, Walsall, Stafford, Stone & Newcastle.

LIVERPOOL The Aurora, every day except Sundays, at ½ past one o'clock sleeping at Birmingham.

MANCHESTER The Traveller, every day except Sundays, at Twelve o'clock, thro' Worcester, Sleeping at Birmingham.

SHEFFIELD The Amity, every day except Sundays, at Twelve o'clock, through Burton, Derby, & Chesterfield.

CHESTER The Dispatch, every day except Sundays, thro' Newport & Fernhill.

BIRMINGHAM The Traveller, thro' Worcester, every day except Sundays, at Twelve o'clock.

BIRMINGHAM The York House Coach, thro' Worcester every day except Sundays, at ½ past One o'clock.

BIRMINGHAM The Mercury, thro' Worcester, every Morning at Eight.

WORCESTER Coaches, every Morning at Eight & Twelve, also at ½ past one o'clock, in the Afternoon.

WOLVERHAMPTON The Everlasting, every Morning at Eight, except Sundays.

COVENTRY The Pilot, thro' Evesham, Alcester, Stratford, Warwick, & Leamington, every day except Sundays, at ½ past one o'clock.

FLY WAGGONS & VANS TO LONDON
on Tuesdays, Thursdays & Saturdays at Twelve o'clock & arrives the following Night

THOMAS HAINES Jun². & Cº. PROPRIETORS.
N³. Every possible comfort & accommodation afforded to those who may be pleased to honour this Establishment with their patronage.
COACHES SENT TO ANY PART OF THE TOWN TO TAKE UP IF REQUIRED.

Cheltenham coach advertisement, c. 1826.

71 *5 March 1787*

THE ORIGINAL
OXFORD and BATH POST-COACH,
Licensed by the Reverend the VICE-CHANCELLOR.
Three times a week.

From the King's-Head, in the Corn Market, Oxford, every Tuesday,
Thursday, and Saturday, at six o'clock in the morning, by way of Witney,
Burford, Cirencester and Tetbury, to the White-Hart, Bath; returns from
Bath every Monday, Wednesday, and Friday, at the same hour. Fare as
usual.

Meets the Salisbury, Southampton, Weymouth, Exeter, and Bristol
Coaches, at Bath; the Falmouth, Plymouth, and Barnstaple Coaches, at
Exeter; and the London Coaches, at Oxford.

Performed to Bath by JOSEPH SPERINCK.

72 *19 December 1796*

A NEW COACH.

To the Gentlemen, Traders, &c. in Bristol, Birmingham, and Glocester.

GENTLEMEN,
As a New Coach has, within these few days, been set up, to carry
passengers between Bristol and Birmingham, it certainly would be greatly
to your advantage to give every encouragement to it. Consider the price
the Proprietors of the old Coaches now charge for every passenger – they
cannot therefore but be greatly alarmed at the setting up of a new Coach,
as it will greatly lessen their income; and, it is said, they are going to lower
the price of travelling considerably, in order, if possible, to cause the
Proprietors of the New Coach to give up their design of continuing it. As
soon as they have gained their ends, and have suppressed the New Coach,
the price of travelling will no doubt be again raised, and perhaps
considerably advanced, and then they will laugh at your folly in being so
easily duped.

AN OLD TRAVELLER.

73 *29 December 1800*

GLOCESTER.

To be Sold by Private Contract, the convenient, extensive, and valuable
Freehold Premises, known by the Name of the Coach Office, in the City of
Glocester, extending from the Northgate-street to Hare-lane; comprizing a
convenient Dwelling-House next the said Street, having two Parlours and
a Counting-House on the Ground Floor, three very convenient Chambers
on the one Pair of Stairs Floor, and a Chamber and Garret in the Upper
Story; detached from the Dwelling-house, and communicating therewith

53

by a covered Passage, is a roomy Kitchen, Pantry, and Brewhouse, with three Cellars under the same, four Chambers and a Dressing-room, above, on the first Floor, and three Garrets over; behind and adjoining to these Buildings is a Coach-yard, Book-keeper's Office, a Granary 45 Feet by 17½ Feet in the Clear, with Coach-houses under and Lofts over the same, and four excellent Stables, with ample Room for 26 Coach or Waggon Horses, a Warehouse, and other Conveniences, with a spacious Gateway for Carriages next Hare-lane. The Land-Tax of the whole has been redeemed. The Premises are not only very eligible for a Coachmaster, but for any Business which requires Room.

For further Particulars enquire of Daniel Turner, Esq., High Wickham, Bucks.

74 *18 October 1802*

Matches against Time. Last week a bet of 120 guineas, between R. Jones, Esq. of Fonmon Castle, Glamorganshire, and Capt. Haskew, of the 15th light dragoons, was determined in favour of the latter gentleman. The match was, that Mr. Jones's chariot, drawn by four horses, should run from the Bell Inn, in this city, to the turnpike leading into Cheltenham (a distance of about ten miles), in forty minutes; but it having been deemed necessary to change horses on the road, the time was exceeded by six minutes and a half.

On Monday last another match was determined between the same parties, in which Mr. Jones betted 650 guineas, that he would travel post from this city to London, with his chariot and four, in ten hours and a half. The distance is about 104 miles. He accordingly started from the Bell at four o'clock in the morning, and, after changing horses eight times, reached Tyburn-turnpike at one o'clock – an hour and a half within the time stipulated – being at the rate of 11½ miles per hour, exclusive of unavoidable stoppages at the different stages. The task, we understand, was performed without difficulty; and Mr. Jones is thus amply recompensed for his want of success in the first bet.

75 *23 May 1803*

OLD COACH-OFFICE, GLOCESTER
CHEAP TRAVELLING.
A COACH

Will set out for London This Day, at One o'clock precisely, and continue every day in the week, at the following

Fares:–

Inside	. . .	£1 10 0
Outside	. . .	15 0

Performed by the Public's most obedient Servants,

JOHN HEATH, Glocester.
R. WILLIAMS, Oxford.
JOHN WILLAN, London.

Glocester, Saturday, May 7, 1803.

BOOTH-HALL INN, GLOCESTER.
LONDON POST-COACH,
Through

CHELTENHAM,	WITNEY,
NORTHLEACH,	OXFORD, And
BURFORD,	HIGH-WYCOMBE

To the BOLT-IN-TUN INN,
FLEET-STREET, LONDON;

Sets out from the above Inn, every Monday, Wednesday, and Friday, at One o'clock, and returns from the Bolt-in-Tun, every Sunday, Tuesday, and Thursday, at the same hour.

Fare, to London, Inside £1 14s. Outside 16s.

N.B. Calls coming in and going out of London, at the Dolphin, oposite Moore's Green-Man-and-Still, Oxford-street, where Parcels will be carefully Booked for this Coach.

Performed by PARKER, CARTER, & Co.

76   *15 July 1811*

(in an advertisement for the 'Telegraph' coach from Gloucester to Leicester)

As the Telegraph was the first Coach started on the Leicester Road, it is sincerely hoped the Public will give the Proprietors that encouragement their endeavours shall deserve; and as there is a powerful opposition formed against their interest, with a threat to run them off the Road, the Proprietors hope the Public will be upon their guard, by ordering all Packages and Parcels by the above Coaches.

77   *1 February 1813*

CAUTION TO COACHMEN and GUARDS.

We whose Names are hereunto subscribed, being the Proprietors of different Mails and other Coaches, in consequence of the daily Impositions and Frauds practised upon us by some of our Coachmen and Guards in taking up Passengers and Parcels, and carrying them from Place to Place, without rendering an Account of the Fares so taken and obtained for the same, but fraudulently converting them to their own use, Do hereby give Notice, that from and after the Date hereof, we are determined to prosecute every Coachman and Guard that we shall find out or discover to

55

be guilty of any of the Offences aforesaid, to the utmost Extremity. And in order the more effectually to prevent such nefarious Practices and Impositions, and to detect the same, we do hereby offer a Reward of Ten Guineas, to be paid (upon conviction) to any Person or Persons who shall give such Information as shall lead to the conviction of any such Offender or Offenders. As witness our Hands this 19th day of December, 1812,

W. Waddell, Plimley, & Co.	John Jones,
H. Evett and Co.	Thomas Wells,
John Hart and Co.	William Fieldhouse,
For Messrs. Willan and Co.	Joseph Davis,
Samuel Johnson,	John Ridler,
Amos Packwood and Co.	John Spencer,
Michael Cutwick,	John Heath.

78 *19 June 1820*

(in an advertisement for the 'Traveller' coach from Bristol to Manchester through Gloucester)

And as the Party who have monopolized the Road, by which the Fares have been kept up, (notwithstanding the reduced price of Hay and Corn,) threaten to oppose this undertaking by every means they can suggest, and have already altered their Six o'clock Coach to go at the same hour as this; it is not doubted but a liberal Public will properly appreciate the object, and give the Traveller their cordial support . . .

79 *14 May 1821*

To COACHMASTERS and INNKEEPERS.

Wanted to unite with a respectable Body of Coachmasters, a few good and indefatigable Partners, between Gloucester, Carmarthen, and Swansea &c. to Work a Coach from those Places to London, the Ground from London to Gloucester being already filled up.

Any Partner understanding the Business well, and having time to devote to the Undertaking in Wales, will be liberally and annually reimbursed for his trouble. It is proposed to work this concern by very short Stages Up and Down, and the advantages to be derived by Welch Partners are not to be had by any other line, namely, to share from end to end.

Further information may be known, by addressing Mr. James Neyler, Plough Hotel, Cheltenham, post-paid.

80 *21 January 1822*

SPENCER'S GENERAL COACH OFFICE
BOOTH-HALL INN,
Westgate-Street, Gloucester.

The Public are respectfully informed, that the following LIGHT POST COACHES, (carrying four insides only), leave the above Office:

LONDON DAY COACH, (The REGULATOR,) through Cheltenham and Oxford, every morning, at a quarter before six, to Brown's Gloucester Warehouse, Oxford-Street, corner of Park-Street, and to the White Horse Cellar, Piccadilly, and Bolt-in-Tun, Fleet-Street, London, by eight the same evening: leaves London every morning at six, and arrives in Gloucester by eight same evening.

CARMARTHEN DAY COACH, (The REGULATOR,) every morning except Sunday, at a quarter before five, thro' Ross, Monmouth, Abergavenny, Brecon, Landovery, and Landilo, to the White Lion and Bush Inns, Carmarthen, early same evening; returns every morning at five, and arrives in Gloucester by nine.

TENBY and PEMBROKE POST COACH, Tuesday Thursday, and Saturday mornings, at five.

SHREWSBURY POST COACH, every afternoon, except Sunday, at three o'clock, through Hereford, Leominster, and Ludlow, to the Lion Inn, Shrewsbury, where it meets the Holyhead Mail and Day Coaches.

HEREFORD POST COACH, through Newent and Ross, every afternoon, except Sunday, at three o'clock, to the Greyhound Inn, Hereford, by eight; returns every morning at five, and arrives in Gloucester by nine, where it meets Coaches to Bath, Bristol, also to Cheltenham, Oxford, &c.

BATH POST COACH, every Monday, Wednesday, and Friday, at a quarter before ten; and every Tuesday, Thursday, and Saturday, at a quarter after nine.

BRISTOL POST COACH, (The PHOENIX,) every morning at nine, Sunday excepted, to the White Hart, Broad-Street.

BRISTOL POST COACH, (The WELLINGTON,) every day at three o'clock, to the White Lion and Bush Coach Offices, Bristol.

BIRMINGHAM POST COACH, (The WELLINGTON,) through Tewkesbury and Worcester, every morning at a quarter past eleven, to the Castle and Saracen's Head Inns, Birmingham.

LIVERPOOL POST COACH, every morning at a quarter-past eleven, to the Saracen's Head Inn, Dale-Street, Liverpool.

SWANSEA POST COACH, thro' Newnham, Chepstow, Newport, Cardiff, and Cowbridge, every Tuesday, Thursday, and Saturday, morning at five o'clock, to the Mackworth Arms Inn, Swansea.

CHELTENHAM COACHES, every morning at a quarter before six, and at nine, every evening at two and half-past two o'clock, to the Plough, Royal, and George Hotels.

Performed by JOHN SPENCER and Co.

The Mail Coaches

A major development in road transport within this period was the introduction of the mail coaches to replace the mounted post-boys who had formerly carried the mail. Originated on an experimental basis by

57

BELL INN,

JOHN PHILLPOTTS, and Co.
CONTRACTORS for conveying the

M A I L

From *London* to *Glocefter, Hereford,*
and all Parts of *South Wales,*
Refpectfully inform the PUBLIC, that their

NEW and ELEGANT

Mail Coaches,

Are now eftablifhed

BY GOVERNMENT AUTHORITY,

WITH A GUARD,

Whereby PERSONS and PROPERTY
are fecurely protected.

And will fet out from the above INN every day at four o'clock,
to the Glocefter Coffee-Houfe, and the Angel St. Clement's
London, where they arrive the next morning at feven.
They return from London every evening at eight o'clock,
and arrive at Glocefter the next day at eleven, from whence
they are continued on to HEREFORD every day, and to
SOUTH WALES as under:

Sundays, Wednefdays, and Fridays

Through ROSS and HEREFORD, to the HAY, BRECK-
NOCK, TRECASTLE, LANDOVERY, LANDILO,
CARMARTHEN, and MILFORD.

Tuefdays, Thurfdays, and Saturdays,

To NEWNHAM, CHEPSTOW, NEWPORT, CAR-
DIFF, COWBRIDGE, NEATH, SWANSEA, and
CARMARTHEN.
They return to GLOCESTER the alternate DAYS at
two o'clock, from whence they proceed to LONDON as
above.
FARE from HEREFORD to LONDON 1l. 16s.
From GLOCESTER, SWANSEA, CARMARTHEN,
and MILFORD as ufual, and from the intermediate ftages
in proportion.

Briftol, Bath, Worcefter and *Birmingham*
Coaches from the above INN every day.

Lot 5. All that MESSUAGE or TENEMENT, with
the garden and premifes thereunto belonging, and now in the
poffeffion of Ifaac Boulton, as tenant thereof.
Lot 6. And alfo all that MESSUAGE or TENEMENT,
and premifes thereunto belonging, in the poffeffion of Ezekiah
Hinton.
The above premifes are freehold, fituate at Avening, in
this county, and are in good condition.
For further particulars apply to the faid Mr. Rodway, at
Avening aforefaid, to Mr. Cox, of Cherrington ; or to Meffrs.
Bowdler and Hofkins, attornies, at Tetbury ; who are au-
horized to treat for the fame.

The London, Cirencefter, Stroud, and
Tetbury

Mail Coaches,

Protected by Government Authority,

With a GUARD,

To carry FOUR infide PASSENGERS

To CIRENCESTER from the above INN, and the Glocefter Coffee-Houfe, Piccadilly, every evening at eight
o'clock, Sundays excepted, and from the King's Head, Cirencefter, every evening at fix o'clock, Saturday excepted.
—Fare to London, 1l. 1s.

The Stroud Mail,

From the above INN, and the Glocefter Coffee-Houfe,
Piccadilly, every Monday, Wednefday, and Friday even-
ings, at eight o'clock ; and returns from the George Inn,
Stroud, every Sunday, Tuefday, and Thurfday, at half
paft three o'clock in the afternoon.—Fare to London,
1l. 5s.

The Tetbury Mail,

From the above INN, and the Glocefter Coffee-Houfe,
Piccadilly, every Tuefday, Thurfday, and Saturday even-
ings, at eight o'clock, and returns from the White Hart,
Tetbury, every Monday, Wednefday, and Friday, at four
o'clock in the afternoon.—Fare from Tetbury 1l. 5s.
PLACES and PARCELS regularly booked at the White
Hart, Tetbury ; the King's Head, Cirencefter ; George
Inn, Stroud ; New Inn, Letchlade ; Crown, Pufey-Furze ;
and Lamb Inn, Abington.
☞ The Proprietors will not be accountable for any par-
cel above FIVE POUNDS value, unlefs entered as fuch,
and paid for accordingly.
Performed by C. IBBERSON, London. ?
J. SAVAGE, Tetbury. ⎰ And Co.

Gloucester Journal advertisement for London mailcoaches in 1785, the year that
they first ran from Gloucestershire. The contract for the Gloucester coaches was
at first awarded to a partnership which included the landlord of the King's Head
inn but was soon afterwards transferred to his rival, John Phillpotts of the Bell.

John Palmer on the London-Bath road in 1784 (no. 81), they were introduced in the succeeding year on most of the principal mail-routes, including that through Gloucester to Wales. The new system was organized as a series of partnerships between the Post Office and local coachmasters. The coachmasters contracted to convey the mail over a particular stretch of road, provided the driver and horses, and carried passengers in the coaches on their own account; the Post Office provided the armed guards, while the coaches, built to a standard design, were supplied and leased to the contractors by a firm of London coachmakers under a monopoly right granted by the Post Office. The division of responsibility between the Post Office and the coachmaster is shown in no. 84, while nos. 85–6 illustrate the overriding duty laid upon the guard of getting his mailbag to its destination, if necessary abandoning the coach and continuing by other means. (For a detailed account of the mail-coach system, see J. Copeland, *Roads and their Traffic*, 1968, pp. 109–131).

'The dispatch and continuance of the conveyance of the Mail by coaches, from Bristol to Milford-Haven, in the course of the correspondence with Ireland, (is) of the greatest importance to the parts of South Wales, thro' which it passes . . .' This statement prefaced a notice placed in the *Journal* of 19 October 1789, calling for a meeting at Swansea to consider the setting up of an association for the prosecution of parishes and trusts which failed in their responsibilities for keeping up any part of the route. To be on a mail-coach route was a matter of significance to a provincial town, contributing to its economy, bolstering its sense of its own importance, and bringing its inhabitants their earliest news of national and international events (no. 87). The townspeople of Abingdon in Berkshire (no. 83) felt annoyed and slighted by the decision of John Palmer (who had become Surveyor of Mails) to make the Wycombe–Oxford–Burford road the mail coach route to Gloucester rather than the Abingdon–Faringdon–Lechlade road. The latter road, which the Abingdon burgesses still referred to as 'the great Gloucestershire road', had once been the main London to Gloucester route but had been gradually ousted from that position by the Oxford route as coach travel developed during the 18th century.

81 *16 August 1784*

Bath, Aug. 11.
The New Mail Coach has travelled with an expedition that has been really astonishing, having seldom exceeded thirteen hours in going or returning from London. It is made very light, carries four passengers, and runs with

a pair of horses, which are changed every six or eight miles; and as the bags at the different offices on the road are made up against its arrival, there is not the least delay. The guard rides with the coachman on the box, and the mail is deposited in the boot. By this means, the Inhabitants of this city and Bristol have the London letters a day earlier than usual.

82 *29 August 1785*

Glocester, August 27.
GLOUCESTER MAIL COACHES
Persons and Property protected
By Government Authority
With a Guard

The Proprietors of the above Coaches, having agreed to convey the Mail to and from London and Gloucester, with a Guard for its protection, respectfully inform the public, that they are constructed so as to accommodate four inside passengers in the most commodious manner, and will set off every evening at eight o'clock, from the Bolt and Tun Inn, Fleet-Street, and the Gloucester Coffee-House, in Piccadilly, London, and arrive at the King's Head Inn, Glocester, the next morning; also from the King's Head Inn, Glocester, every afternoon at four o'clock, and arrive at the Bolt and Tun Inn, Fleet-Street, London, the next morning.

The price for each inside passenger to London, 1l. 8s. Parcels will be immediately forwarded, and punctually delivered agreeable to the directions.

Performed by
WILLIAM HARRIS, London,
JAMES WILLIAMS, Oxford.
ISAAC THOMPSON ⎫
and   ⎬ Glocester.
Messrs. PAINS,   ⎭

83 *16 January 1792*

BOROUGH OF ABINGDON, Jan. 5.

At a Meeting of the principal Inhabitants and Traders of the above place, to take into consideration, the result of an application to Mr Palmer, for a participation of the benefits derived from Mail Coaches, and to prevent the delay and uncertainty now attending the conduct of the Mail, to and from Abingdon, and many other places; the following resolutions were unanimously agreed to.

First, That the mode of conveying the Mail by horses and bags, between Oxford and this place, and down the Western road to the lower part of Berkshire, part of Glocestershire, North Wiltshire, Bath and Bristol, is uncertain, dilatory, injurious to commerce, and more hazardous than before the adoption of Mr. Palmer's plan.

Secondly, That the neglect of Mr. Palmer, in giving no answer to the official representation of our chief Magistrate, leaves us no room to hope for redress from that quarter.

Thirdly, That the Gentlemen and Traders of the vale of Berkshire, and of all other places interested, be requested to concur with the inhabitants of this town, in applications to his Majesty's Post Master General for redress.

Fourthly, That no sufficient reason appears, why the Mail is not conveyed down the great Gloucestershire road as usual.

Fifthly, That benefits, partially conferred and precariously held, ought not to be accepted as an adequate performance of a plan, which pretends to effect a general reform, and is held out as a national advantage.

Sixthly, That these resolutions be printed in the London Evening and General Evening Posts; and in the Oxford, Reading, Glocester, and Bristol papers.

EDWARD CHILD, Chairman.

84 *11 November 1811*

The Guard of the Gloucester and Hereford Mail Coach, has been dismissed the service, by order of the Inspector of Mail Coaches, and the Coachman by the Proprietor of the Coach, for behaving in a very abusive manner to a lady and another female passenger, the week before last, on the road from Gloucester to Ledbury.

85 *24 January 1814*

The inclemency of the weather continues with unabated rigour. Some of the principal roads from this city are completely choaked up, and rendered impassable, even on horseback, by drifts of snow of immense height; and the inconvenience, being general, is severely felt by the commercial world, from the stoppage of intercourse. The London Mails due here on Thursday and Friday, only arrived about three in the afternoons of Saturday and yesterday, brought the principal part of the way on horseback by the mail-guards, who had many hair-breadth escapes (one of them having been four times dug out of the snow) on this perilous service . . .

86 *31 January 1814*

On Wednesday the wind came round to the South, and a fine gentle thaw succeeded . . . The London mails due here on the Saturday and Sunday were brought in together on Monday evening; and those in succession have regularly arrived on the days due, about three or four hours later than the customary time. The mail-coach has again commenced running; but it is still obliged to be worked with six horses. It ought in Justice to be noticed, that it has been owing to the persevering exertions of the guards attached to the London and Welsh mails through this city, that the cessation of intercourse with the capital was not of much longer duration – these men having performed the journies on horseback with the greatest difficulty and personal danger; and we hope their meritorious conduct will not pass unrewarded.

87   *11 April 1814*

The London mail, for several days last week, was profusely decorated with laurel and ribbon, on its arrival in this city, in manifestation of the glorious news it conveyed (*i.e. the abdication of Bonaparte*). It was followed through the streets by hundreds of people, and cheered in its progress by the heartfelt gratulations of all ranks . . .

88   *18 July 1814*

A meeting of the innkeepers who horse the mail-coach between this city and Milford, was lately held at Avery's Hotel, Monmouth, when, by a new arrangement, that respectable body of Proprietors agreed with his Majesty's Postmaster General, that the coach from London shall reach Milford two hours earlier than by the former contract. A similar meeting has also taken place at the Black Rock Inn, Monmouthshire, for the regulation of the mail on that road, by which the Proprietors engaged that it shall arrive at Carmarthen every morning at five minutes past seven o'clock. These arrangements are felt to be a great accomodation in so far as they afford an additional space of more than two hours between the arrival and departure of the London mails.

Rival Coaches: The 'Union' versus 'Masters'

One feature of the early 19th century, as an increasing number of coaches came on the roads, was the fierce competition between operators on the same route. The extracts printed below concern the rivalry and price-cutting war between two firms operating on the Stroud to London route. Stroudwater Union Patent Coaches, a new firm established in 1807 by a large group of shareholders from the Stroud area, challenged the old-established coach which had been run for more than thirty years by the Masters family of Cirencester with various London partners (cf. *G.J.* 4 Apr. 1774; 14 Nov. 1796). Some account of the contest is given by P.H. Fisher (*Stroud*, pp. 109–11); he attributed the failure of the two successive Stroud Union companies, with the loss of some £7,000 in the project, partly to bad management by the inexperienced committee of shareholders who ran the business. Fisher also gives some details of the patent safety coach mentioned in no. 89. It had a large luggage boot underneath, on which were four small wheels designed to keep the coach upright if a wheel came off, a common cause of accidents: 'The patentee was, doubtless, desirous of proving its practical safety, and this was accordingly effected; for, soon after it began to run, I was sitting on the front of the coach one night on a journey to Town, and suddenly, found the part of it whereon I sat, sink down; but the shock was slight, and we moved on for a short space, without damage or any inconvenience. One of the fore-wheels had fallen off. It was not discovered at the time, by what agency this had been effected, though I surmised it, and the wheel being sought for and found, was re-adjusted, and we proceeded on our way'.

89 *1 June 1807*

STROUD-WATER
UNION PATENT COACHES.

The Public are respectfully informed, that the Stroud-Water Union Patent Coaches, will start from the King's Arms Inn, Stroud-Water, to run through Woodchester, Nailsworth, Hampton, Cirencester, Fairford, Lechlade, Faringdon, Abingdon, Benson, Henley, Maidenhead, Colnbrook, Slough, Hounslow, and Brentford, to London, on Monday, the 1st day of June, 1807, at Eleven o'clock in the Forenoon; and for Stroud-Water through the above-mentioned places, from the Angel Inn, Angel-Street, St.Martin's-le-Grand, London, the same day, at half past Three o'clock in the Afternoon; and continue to run daily, at the above-mentioned hours, from the above places.

As these Coaches are established solely for the accomodation of the Public, and as no expence has been spared in purchasing Milton's Patent Coaches, which cannot be overturned without the most wilful neglect; and as the Proprietors have been careful to engage sober and steady Coachmen and Guards, they hope they shall have the favour and support of the Public in proportion to their endeavours to please.

Inside Fare, 1*l*. 8*s*.: Outside, 16*s*.: and all intermediate places in the same proportion. Luggage, 1*d*. per lb. Inside passengers allowed to carry 14 lbs. luggage . . .

The Proprietors . . . invite a candid consideration of the principles upon which their claims are founded. The Union Coach is established to promote not private but public advantage; and the conduct of the Proprietors will be regulated by considerations of general utility alone. They therefore take this opportunity to declare that they are actuated by no motives of personal hostility; and that though they will not suffer themselves to be deterred from their duty to the Public by any opposition whatever, yet they are desirous of cautioning those to whom they look for support, against any attempt that may be made to delude, by holding out

The Bull and Mouth inn, St. Martins-le-Grand, one of the London inns used as a terminus by Gloucestershire coaches.

temporary advantages, in the hope of future emolument. It is the intention of the Proprietors of the Union Coach, that its accomodations be in all respects *safe* and *comfortable*, and the charges as moderate as possible.

90 *8 June 1807*

The Old London, Cirencester, Tetbury, and Stroud-Water Coaches, with a Guard throughout, set out from the Golden Heart Inn, Stroud, every day (except Saturday) at half-past Eleven o'Clock; from The Salutation, Hampton, at half-past Twelve; and from the Swan Inn, Cirencester, at Two o'Clock; to the Bull and Mouth Inn, Bull and Mouth-street, London; and return from thence every afternoon (except Saturday) at Four o'Clock; at the following reduced prices:-

	Inside.	Outside.
To and from London and Stroud	£1 5 0	£0 14 0
Tetbury and Hampton	1 3 0	0 13 0
Cirencester	1 1 0	0 12 0

Luggage One Penny per Pound . . .
WILLAN, MASTERS, and Co. Proprietors.

A Coach to London from the Three Cups Inn, Tetbury, every Sunday, Tuesday, and Thursday, at Twelve o'Clock.

91 *12 October 1807*

The Proprietors of The Stroud-Water Union Coaches, Respectfully return Thanks to a generous Public for the very liberal support they have hitherto experienced; and are happy to find that the principles upon which their Coaches were established are recognized and approved. Encouraged by the most respectable patronage, they assure their Friends that the difficulties arising from opposition and inexperience will only call into action new and surmounting energies. They bid defiance to the secret stratagems incessantly at work to undermine, and to the open violence which caused a temporary interruption of their plan for public accomodation. These stratagems and that violence have served chiefly to excite more general attention; and will spread still wider the disposition for popular association against the impositions of the road . . .

92 *25 January 1808*

REDUCED FARES!!
Stroud-Water Union Coaches.

The Proprietors of the Union Coaches having seen with regret that their endeavours to avoid the appearance of Opposition, have not been duly appreciated by those whom they are reluctantly compelled to consider as their opponents; and regarding themselves as fairly at issue with the Parties who have asserted that theirs shall be the "Cheapest Travelling" – have, at a

General Meeting, unanimously resolved that the Union Coach Fares shall from this time be and continue as low as those of their Competitors.

The Proprietors request their Friends and the Public to accept of grateful acknowledgements for the very liberal support given to their establishment; and beg leave to assure them that, whilst their charges shall be as low as those of any other Coach, their Accommodations shall in all respects be adapted to promote the safety and comfort of those by whom they are patronized.

The above Coaches set out from the King's-Arms Inn, Stroud-water, at Eleven o'Clock in the Morning, and from the Angel Inn, Angel-street, St. Martin's-le-Grand, London, at Three in the Afternoon, every day, except Saturday.

Present Fares as Follow:

	Inside.	Outside.
Stroud to London	£1 5 0	£0 14 0
Hampton ditto	1 3 0	0 14 0
Cirencester ditto	1 0 0	0 12 0
Fairford ditto	0 18 0	0 10 0
Leachlade ditto	0 17 0	0 10 0
Farringdon ditto	0 16 0	0 9 0
Abingdon ditto	0 14 0	0 8 0

And all other places in proportion.

N.B. Parcels and Passengers booked at the Angel Inn, and Glocester Coffee-House, London; King's Arms, Stroud; George, Nailsworth; Hampton, Cirencester, &c.

Stroud, January 20, 1808.

93 *14 March 1808*

Cheap Travelling, at Reduced Prices,
The LONDON,
CIRENCESTER, and STROUDWATER
COACHES,

Continue to set out from the Bull and Mouth Inn, London, every Afternoon; and from the Golden Heart Inn, Stroud, every Morning, except Saturday, at Eleven o'Clock. Fares – Inside, 1l. 4s. Outside, 13s.

WILLAN, MASTERS, and Co. Proprietors

The above Coaches call at the Old and New White-Horse Cellars, in Piccadilly.

94 *27 June 1808*

STROUD UNION COACHES.

Notice is hereby given, That this Concern is Dissolved, and that all Demands upon the same, up to this day, are to be transmitted to the Union Coach Office, Stroud, within 21 days from the date hereof.

The Proprietors take this occasion of informing the Public, that the Union Coaches will be continued as usual, by the newly associated Proprietors, upon the same principles of public spirit and accomodation as have hitherto characterized the concern; and beg leave to recommend them to the support of a discerning Public.
Stroud, June 27, 1808.

95 *12 June 1809*

SALE of Capital COACH HORSES.
STROUD, GLOCESTERSHIRE.

To be Sold by Auction, at the King's Arms Inn, in Stroud, on Friday, the 23d day of June, 1809, at Eleven o'Clock;-
About Fifty Capital Seasoned Coach Horses, mostly young, and in high condition; now working the Union Coach, between London and Stroudwater. As they will be sold without reserve, and are allowed to be equal to any Coachers in the Kingdom, and many of them well matched and suited for Gentlemen's Carriages, it cannot be doubted but the public attention will be excited in proportion to the probable advantages resulting from such an opportunity of purchasing.

Stroud, June 9, 1809.

96 *19th June 1809*

CONTINUATION OF THE
Stroudwater, Tetbury & Wotton-under-Edge
UNION COACHES.

The Third Associated Body of Proprietors of the above Coaches, most earnestly solicit the patronage and support of their Friends and the Public in general. They are unwilling to make professions, but hope their arrangements will merit and experience due encouragement.
The Union will continue to run from the Bell Savage, Ludgate Hill, London, every Monday, Wednesday, and Saturday Afternoon, at Half-past Two o'Clock; and from the King's Arms, Stroud, every Sunday, Tuesday, and Thursday, at Twelve o'Clock; and from the Swan, Wotton, at Eleven o'Clock.
Performed by Hayward, Prockter, & Co. Stroudwater, June 12, 1809.

LONDON, CIRENCESTER,
STROUDWATER, TETBURY, AND KINGSCOTE
ROYAL MAIL COACHES.

The Public are respectfully informed, That the above Mail Coaches will set out from the Bull and Mouth Inn, London, every Evening at Six o'Clock;

from the Golden Heart, Stroudwater, and Kirkby's Hotel, Kingscote, every Afternoon.

Also, a Telegraph Coach, from the Bull and Mouth Inn, London, every Monday, Wednesday, and Friday Afternoon; and returns from the Golden Heart, Stroudwater, Tuesday, Thursday, and Sunday, at Noon; and from the Swan Inn, Cirencester, at Two o'Clock.

Performed by WILLAN, MASTERS, & COSTAR.

CHAPTER FOUR
Carriers

Packhorse and Wagon

Almost as regular advertisers in the *Journal* as the coach proprietors were the long-distance carriers of goods. Carriers' wagons had been seen on the roads since medieval times and probably predominated in the carrying trade by the start of the period, but on some major routes strings of packhorses were found more convenient until the middle years of the 18th century when the turnpike trusts at last began to have a significant effect on the condition of the roads (nos. 97, 101, 104). William Good, who in the Newent area operated over some of the most notorious roads of the county, was probably one of the last carriers to use packhorses over any distance. Subsequently pack animals were relegated to very local use: for coal-carrying in the Forest of Dean; for moving cloth and wool between clothier's mill and weaver's cottage in the Stroud valleys; and for taking farm produce to market. Farmers in the Bishop's Cleeve area, for example, used packhorses to take their corn to Tewkesbury market until the 1780s (Bennett, *Tewkes.* p. 278*n*).

During the 18th century Gloucester usually had one or two carriers running services to London and Bristol, while the London wagons from Hereford and South Wales were a familiar sight in the city as they rumbled up Westgate Street to an overnight stop at one of the inns. Carriers were not, however, as vital to Gloucester as they were to inland places of comparative size, because of the use made of the river Severn for the transport of goods. The trows passing up and down river provided a cheaper and more convenient, though less safe, conveyance for bulk goods to Bristol and the Midlands (no. 100), while the little river ports below Gloucester, like Gatcombe and Newnham, provided the city's tradesmen with coasting services to London and South Wales. The advertisements in the *Journal* reveal that the more substantial market towns of the county also had their London (and sometimes Bristol) waggoners by the later years of the 18th century. Much less frequently do we learn from its pages anything of the many local carriers and hauliers: those who connected small country places with the nearest market town (nos. 108, 114); those who distributed Staffordshire coal inland from Tewkesbury and other places on the river (no. 105); and those who hauled timber from the Forest of Dean to the riverside (no. 115).

Long-distance carrying by road in the 18th century was a slow and tedious business. The time of four or five days from Gloucester to London taken in the 1720s by the lumbering covered wagons with their four or five horses pulling in line was hardly improved on before the end of the century (nos. 98, 110). Only in the early years of the 19th century were the 'flying wagons' of such operators as Tanner and Baylis able to cut the time appreciably; and at that period, as with the coaches, a keen element of competitiveness was introduced to the business (no. 116).

The men who ran the wagon services were sometimes in business in quite a big way, owning a substantial stable of horses and wagons, but it was not a trade that brought them great wealth and status. The profit margin was apparently small and the risks could be great, as Rowland Heane of Gloucester found only a few months after taking over the business of his old employer Samuel Manning (no. 109; cf. *G.J.* 26 Feb. 1787). When Thomas Masters, a Cirencester to London carrier, died in 1799, his widow, announcing that she would continue the business, described it as 'the only means of subsistence for a numerous family' (*G.J.* 30 Sept. 1799). It was a trade in which bankruptcies occurred fairly frequently (e.g. *G.J.* 26 Dec. 1763; 10 June 1782; 7 Mar. 1796).

97 *13 December 1726*

Notice is hereby given, That Tho. Madocke, the Bristol and Worcester Carrier from Gloucester, proposes to sell his Drift of Pack-horses, with several good Hackneys, at a Reasonable Rate.

Note, Any Person that will buy the whole, or any Part of them, and will continue in his Business, may be furnish'd with a Warehouse, Stable, Hay, and other Conveniences.

98 *1 April 1729*

This is to give Notice,
That Robert Arnold of the City of Gloucester,
WAGGONER,
(having purchased the Custom and Business
of Mr. John Wood, lately deceas'd)

Continues to keep the usual and constant Stage between this City and London; and carries all manner of Goods, Wares, Merchandizes, and Passengers, at reasonable Rates; and sets out from his own House in the North-Gate-street in Gloucester, on Tuesday the first of April, by Three in the Morning, and goes into the King's-Head in the Old Change, on Friday following; and sets out from thence on Saturday morning, about Eleven a Clock, and returns into Gloucester the Wednesday following.

Whoever hath any Goods to be carried below Gloucester, (where no Stage goes through) upon an Agreement made at his own House in Gloucester, or at his Inn in London aforesaid, the same will be safely deliver'd.

And as Mr. Wood formerly kept a Waggon to Ledbury, during the Summer-season, the same will, upon Incouragement, be continued.

Perform'd, if GOD permit,

By ROBERT ARNOLD.

N.B. No Plate, Money, Jewels, Writings or Bonds, pack'd up in any Box, Trunk, Portmanteau, &c. will be taken in Charge, without Notice thereof given to R.A.

Likewise a very good Hearse and Harness to be Lett or Sold. And also good Saddle Horses to be Lett.

99   *16 July 1734*

Notice is hereby given,

That for the Benefit of the Forest-Division only, upon Tuesday the 13th of August next, will be given a Piece of Plate five Pounds Value, to be run for at a Place call'd Crump-Meadow, near the middle of the Forest of Dean, by any Horse, &c. that has carried Coals, Mine or Oar, constantly within the said Forest Division for 6 Months past, and that never won a Plate of that Value before, the best of 3 Heats, 3 times round at each Heat, carrying ten Stone . . .

100   *24 February 1736*

An unfair Practice has been discover'd among several Carriers that travel to and from this City (*i.e. Bristol*), who, after an Agreement for a certain Sum of Money per Hund. Weight for Carriage of Goods by Land, have clandestinely put such Goods on board the Trows bound up Severn, Avon, Stratford, &c. whereby they defraud the Traders, who, for Security of their Goods, pay a good Price for Land-Carriage, when at the same Time they might send them in those Trows 3 4ths cheaper, which the Carriers have put in their own Pockets, as tho' they had carry'd the Goods themselves. One of these Carriers is like to come off but indifferently on this Score, he having put six Packs of Cloth, to the Value of 400l. belonging to Mess. Smith and Martin of Chipping Cambden, on board Mr. Harrison's Trow that was lost in the Storm.

101   *30 July 1745*

This is to give Notice,

That John Restell, Carrier, who now keeps the Pack-Horse Inn, near the Market-Place in Tewksbury, in the County of Gloucester, (where all

Packhorses with bales of cloth or wool, passing Avening church.

Gentlemen, Tradesmen, &c. will meet with good Accomodations) has fixed his Stages, in the following Manner, for his Pack-Horses, viz. He sets out every Monday Morning from Tewksbury, dines the same Day at the White-Hart in Gloucester, and reaches the Upper-Crown in Newport the same Night. Every Tuesday he arrives at the Horse-shoe in Wine-Street, Bristol; and the same Day reaches the Angel in Bath, kept by James Maggs, Carrier. Returns every Wednesday to the Horse-shoe in Bristol, and to Newport the same Night; and to Gloucester, and his own House in Tewksbury, every Thursday; and to the Bell and Unicorn in Worcester, every Friday. He likewise carries Goods to Birmingham and Wolverhampton, or any Parts of the North.

All Merchants Goods, Packs, Parcels or Passengers will be carried at very reasonable Rates; also any Person may be furnish'd with Double or Single Horses, very reasonably.

Perform'd, with good able Horses, (if God permit) by me,

JOHN RESTELL.

N.B. He keeps his own Stages as usual.

102 *28 August 1750*

This is to give NOTICE,

That William Mountain hath removed his Waggons from the Bell Inn in Friday-street to the George Inn on Snow-Hill, London; who carries Goods and Passengers as follows: By the Monmouth Waggons to all Parts of South-Wales, viz. Monmouth, Abergavenny, Brecon, Glamorganshire, Landovery, Landilo, Carmarthen, Pembroke, Haverfordwest, and all Places adjacent; these Waggons likewise carry for Cheltenham, &c. and go through Huntley, Mitchel-Deane, and Coleford: And by the other Waggons, to Hampton-Road, Chalford, Bisley, Cirencester, Fairford, Letchlade, Farringdon, and Places adjacent. Perform'd (if God permit) by

WM. MOUNTAIN . . .

103 *1 April 1755*

Glocester, Jan. 11.

SAMUEL MANNING

Gives Notice to all Gentlemen, Tradesmen, and Others, That he has purchased the London Stage-Waggons of the Widow Arnold, late Carrier, and will set out from his own House, at the Nag's-head in the Upper Northgate-street, on Tuesday Morning early, (and so continue Once a Fortnight) and arrive at the King's-head in the Old 'Change, London, on Friday following, return from thence on the Morrow, and be at Glocester the Wednesday after. He goes by Fairford, Letchlade, Farringdon, and Abingdon, where he delivers Goods and Passengers at the lowest Prices N.B. He keeps his Bristol and Worcester Stages as usual, and likewise goes with a Waggon from Glocester to the George in Castle street, Bristol, Once a Week, through Painswick, Stroud, Hampton, and Tetbury, and takes up and delivers Goods at those and all other adjacent Places.

Performed (if GOD permit) by,
Their humble Servant,
SAMUEL MANNING.

He takes no Charge of Money, or Plate, unless entered as such.

104   *15 July 1755*

WILLIAM GOOD

Gives Notice to Gentlemen, Tradesmen, and Others,

That he has Able Horses, which will go from Ledbury thro' Newent to the White-hart in the Southgate-street, Glocester, every Monday and Thursday, and to the Unicorn in Broad-street, Worcester, every Saturday; and will return to Ledbury the same Days: Whoever will please to employ him in carrying Goods and Parcels to the above-mentioned Places may depend on the utmost Care's being taken of them, and the Favour's being greatly acknowledged by,

Their humble Servant,
WM. GOOD.

N.B. He begins his Stage the 4th of August.

105   *18 November 1755*

This is to give Notice,

That at John Leyes's, Hallier, upon the Key, in Tewkesbury, are to be disposed of, as soon as possible, all Things belonging to the Business of a Hallier, as Waggons, Drays, Horses, Geer, Ploughs, and Dray-sledges, by me,

JOHN LEYES.

106   *5 April 1757*

Glocester, April 2.

This is to give Notice,

That a Fish-Cart will set out from the Coach-Office in the Lower Northgate-street every Thursday and Saturday, and will be in London with Fish for Saturday's and Tuesday's Markets, during the Fish-season.

Performed by JOHN TURNER.

107   *15 December 1777*

This is to acquaint Gentlemen, Tradesmen, and others, that the Tewkes-bury, Oxford, and London Flying Stage Waggon, will set out early every Monday Morning from the Maidenhead Inn, in Tewkesbury, and get to London early on Thursday Morning, and return early every Friday

Morning. Calls at the Fleece, in Cheltenham; at Cold Comfort; New Barn; the Greyhound, in Burford; the White Hart, in Witney; Flower-de-Luce, in Oxford; Green Man and Still, Corner of Swallow-Street, Oxford-Road, London; and puts up at the Bell, in Warwick-Lane. Where Goods will be punctually received and delivered at the above Places, by their humble Servants,

J.CHAMBERS, Tewkesbury;
J. JONES, Oxford.

The flying Stage Waggon will not be so long on the Road by two Days as the old Stage Waggon . . .

108 *6 November 1786*

Some merciless villains a few nights ago stole from the stable of William Gill, a poor carrier of Shepscombe, near Painswick, two asses, all his dependence, his daily support . . .

109 28 May 1787

We are sorry to announce to our readers the melancholy accident, which happened early on the Sunday morning the 20th inst. to Mr. Heane's London waggon, between Uxbridge and Gerrard's Cross, loaded with goods for Glocester, as well as a large quantity that were to be forwarded from Glocester to various parts of South Wales, by Mess. Norths, of Brecknock, to the amount, as supposed, of about 2000l. The waggon overturning, and the waggoner taking off the horses, called up at a little cottage a labouring man, to take charge of the waggon, 'till he could procure help from other waggoners, who that night lay at Gerrard's-Cross, about three miles distant; but on his return, he found the waggon, with the whole loading, a few inconsiderable articles excepted, consumed to ashes, occasioned by the man, who was left in charge of it, taking a candle to find out the leakage of a cask of brandy.

The poor fellow, reflecting on what he had done, in the agonies of desperation, the next morning, cut his throat.

We hear Mr. Heane wishes those, who are sufferers by this misfortune, to send in an account of their losses, that he may, by the assistance of his friends, do his utmost to satisfy them, and thereby deserve their future favors. As Mr. Heane had but lately succeeded Mr. Manning in the carrying business, this disaster must be severely felt, without the continuance of those instances of generosity, which have by several of the sufferers been humanely extended to him.

4 June 1787

GLOCESTER.
Rowland Heane's Subscription.

The distressed situation to which Rowland Heane, of this city, Carrier, is

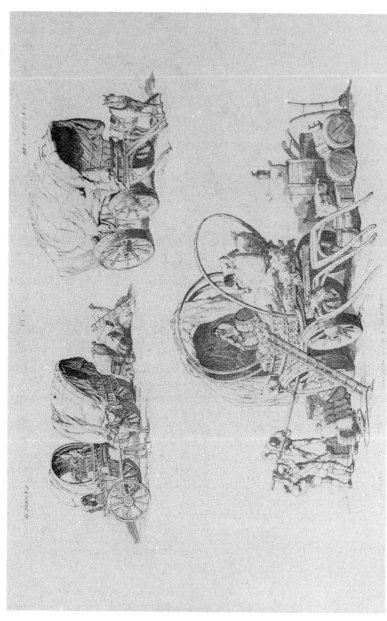

Carriers' wagons in the early 19th century. In the bottom sketch the goods are being packed down tight by means of ropes and a lever.

reduced by the Burning of his Waggon, and its whole Lading, being universally known and regretted, will, it is presumed, (with the request of several respectable Gentlemen) be a sufficient apology for informing the public, that a Subscription is opened for his relief, at the Bank of Mr. John Turner, in Glocester.

When it was considered, that inattention or misconduct on the part of the sufferer, had no share in producing this dreadful calamity, which in its nature is almost without a parallel, and in extent so wide, that, after annihilating the produce of near 20 years hard labour, it still leaves him incumbered with an immense debt, there is no doubt but a generous community, ever ready to assist where real merit labours under misfortunes, will, on this occasion, contribute with their accustomed liberality.

110 *3 October 1791*

London and Glocester Common Stage Waggon.

John Simpson, Carrier, respectfully begs leave to inform his friends and the public, that his Waggon will set out from Kellow's Warehouse, on the Quay, Glocester, every Sunday evening, and will arrive at the Swan-Inn, Holborn Bridge, London, on the Thursday following; returns from thence on the Friday, and arrives at the above warehouse every Wednesday evening.

He takes goods from Cirencester, Fairford, Lechlade, Farringdon, Abingdon, Henly, and the intermediate places . . .

111 *17 November 1806*

To CARRIERS and others.
TO BE SOLD BY AUCTION,
By Mr. WANE,

By Order of the Assignees of Mr. John Simpson, a Bankrupt, on the Premises, at Fairford, in the county of Glocester, on Thursday, Friday, and Saturday, the 20th, 21st, and 22d days of November, 1806;–

All the Broad and Narrow-wheel Waggons, Carts, Horses, Household Goods, and other Effects, of the said Bankrupt; comprising Four Nine-inch-wheel Waggons with Tilts, and One Rolling Waggon; Four Narrow-wheel ditto; Two Broad and Two Narrow-wheel Carts; Twenty-nine Waggon horses, One Nag Horse and a Yearling Colt; Thirty Sets of Harness; One Sow and Pigs, and One ditto in Pig; Rick of English Hay; Roll and Frame; Harrows, Drags, and Ploughs; Two Staddles and Timber; Van and Sieves; Malt and Bean Mill; quantity of Waggon Timber; Withy and Oak Poles; Fire Wood; excellent Beam, Scales, and a large assortment of Lead and Cast-iron Weights; quantity of Dung, and many other articles . . .

112 *8 August 1803*

We understand that the truly spirited and patriotic offer of Mr. Rowland Heane, London carrier, of this city, to supply Government gratuitously with the use of the whole of his waggons and horses, for the public service, has been accepted, and acknowledged in very flattering terms, in a letter from the Secretary to the Board of Ordnance.

113 *26 September 1803*

His Majesty has been pleased to accept the patriotic offer of Mr. Daniel Masters, Jun. of Cirencester, to furnish Government, in case of an invasion, with 70 horses, and a proportionate number of waggons.

114 *21 April 1806*

On Saturday se'nnight died, William Lewis, of Ruscombe, near Stroud, in this county. He had attended Glocester market, as a carrier, upwards of forty years . . .

115 *14 August 1809*

To Timber Haulliers

Wanted, by Bowsher, Hodges, and Watkins, Four Teams of Six Horses each, to haul Timber from Dean Forest to Purton Yard.
    The Timber will be set out in lots, and a liberal price given, and constant work will be warranted for Twelve Months from the date hereof.
    For further Particulars, apply to Mr. John Herbert, Nibley Green, near Blakeney; or at the Counting-House of Messrs. Bowsher and Co. Chepstow. Chepstow, August 2, 1809.

116 *3 January 1814*

WAGGONS REMOVED
From the King's Head Inn, Old 'Change, and
George Inn, Snowhill,
To the Saracen's Head Inn,
Friday-Street, Cheapside, London.

GEO. NORTH and Co's Old Established Waggons, through Mitcheldean, Ross, Colford, Monmouth, Abergavenny, Brecknock, Carmarthen, Pembroke, Haverfordwest, to Milford, with all parts of South Wales, and the South of Ireland, every Tuesday, Thursday, and Saturday.
    JOS. TROKES's (late Morris) Old Established Waggons to Ross, Hereford, Hay, Kington, Leominster, Presteign, Weobly, and all parts of Herefordshire and Radnorshire, every Thursday and Saturday; And
    JAS. HEANE's Old Established Waggons, to Gloucester, Cheltenham, Tewkesbury, Painswick, Dursley, Uley, Ledbury, Northleach, and Burford, Daily.

The Public are respectfully informed, that all Goods, &c. will, in future, be regularly forwarded by the respective Waggons, agreeably to the above Days, from the Saracen's Head Inn, where the greatest Civility, Punctuality, and Dispatch, will be unceasingly observed, and be the best proof of the necessity of the alteration.

And the proprietors of the Conveyances respectfully caution their friends to be very particular in ordering their Correspondents to send and direct their Goods to the Saracen's Head and not to be misled by anonymous hand bills issued announcing Fly and Slow Waggons from the King's Head, Old Change, and George, Snowhill, which are without any foundation, not even a Wheel or Hoof being on the Ground . . .

Serving the Clothing Country

One part of Gloucestershire for which the carriers performed a particularly vital role was the area of clothmaking valleys on the edges of the Cotswolds around Stroud and Dursley. That area required regular communications with London, to carry cloth up to the Blackwell Hall cloth market, and with those neighbouring towns, including Gloucester, Cirencester and Tetbury, whose woolstapling industries supplied the clothiers with their raw material.

Many of the London carriers who served the clothing country over the period were based at Rodborough, which between 1752 and 1814 was on the main Stroud to London road through Cirencester and was a convenient collecting point for goods from the valleys that centred on Stroud. There was also a group of London carriers based in the Horsley and Kingscote area, from which they served Wotton and Dursley and also at times provided Tetbury and Malmesbury with their London services. In the southerly group the families of Shipton and Creed were predominant and in the Rodborough group those of Niblett and Tanner. Four generations of the Tanners ran London wagons from Rodborough, and the early-19th-century representative of the family, Samuel Tanner, formed a successful partnership with A.K. Baylis and instituted a service of fast wagons which got the clothiers' wares to the capital in two days (*V.C.H. Glos.* xi. 230; no. 124). Tanner and Baylis later extended their operations to Gloucester and Cheltenham, taking over the business of the Heane family of Gloucester in 1817 (Counsel, *Gloucester*, p. 245; *G.J.* 28 July 1817).

In a trade notorious for its fluctuating prices it was often of vital importance for the cloth to reach the Blackwell Hall factors within a particular time, and, as no. 121 shows, it was sometimes put on board the faster coaches rather than the carriers' wagons.

TANNER & BAYLIS.

FLY
WAGGONS,
to & from
LONDON.

IN
TWO DAYS
EACH
WAY.

FLY WAGGONS.

EVERY MORNING & EVENING *(Sunday Excepted)* **IN TWO DAYS**
each way conveying Goods to, and from, the
GLOUCESTERSHIRE WAREHOUSE 55 WHITE CROSS STREET CRIPPLEGATE
London
their Warehouses, Winchcomb Street Cheltenham
AND WESTGATE STREET, GLOUCESTER,
and all parts of the Counties of Gloucester Hereford, Monmouth,
and South Wales,
Bath, Bristol, the West, Ireland, &c.
WAGGONS DAILY,
TO & FROM THE BELL INN, THOMAS STREET, BRISTOL,
AND No 20 CORN STREET, BATH.
Conveyances from all parts of the West meet at Bristol
where Goods are also Shipped for Ireland, &c.
Luggage or Goods consigned to Tanner & Baylis
promptly forwarded to any place in England Wales or Scotland
N.B. Not accountable for Package or Parcel above the value of
Five Pounds unless entered as such & paid for accordingly.

TANNER & BAYLIS'S
Regular & Expeditious Fly Vans,

PECULIARLY
ADAPTED
FOR
LUGGAGE &c.

FLY VAN

TO AND FROM
LONDON,
IN 20 HOURS
EACH WAY.

TO & FROM THE
GLOUCESTERSHIRE WAREHOUSE 55 WHITE CROSS ST. CRIPPLEGATE,
London
Every Tuesday, Thursday & Saturday at Noon, arriving at their
Warehouse Winchcomb Street CHELTENHAM in Twenty Hours & at their
Warehouse Westgate Street Gloucester, in Twenty Two hours.

Advertisement by the Gloucestershire carrying firm of Tanner and Baylis, *c.* 1826.

Other advertisements by carriers of the Stroud clothmaking region reflect the importance to its clothiers and other tradesmen of regular links with Gloucester and Bristol. Thomas Gardiner in 1790 had competitors on his routes to both cities from the region (no. 120; *G.J.* 12 July 1790). The important provincial fairs remained another outlet for the clothiers' products until well into the 18th century, as the special excursion laid on to Salisbury fair illustrates (no. 119).

117 *7 August 1750*

NOTICE is hereby given,

That the Constant Stage-Waggons, lately kept by Daniel Niblet, are now continued by Michael Ballard, who carries Goods and Passengers, at reasonable Rates, from Stroudwater, Painswick, Bisley, Hampton, Cirencester, Fairford, Letchlade, Farringdon, and Places adjacent; and that they are removed, from the Bell-Inn in Friday-street, to the George-Inn on Snow-hill, London, where Attendance is given by Richard Forster, Book-keeper, from the said Bell-Inn.

Perform'd, if God permit, by
MICHAEL BALLARD.

118 *18 December 1750*

NOTICE is hereby given, That

The right Malmesbury and Tetbury constant Stage Waggons (late Moses Ball's) are now kept by Thomas Shipton, of Horsley, who continues to carry Goods and Passengers, at the usual Prices, to and from Malmesbury, Tetbury, Charleton, Brinkworth, Gazan, the Lee, Sheston, Pinkney, Didmarton, Shipton, Summerford, Dancey, and all Places adjacent; setting out of Malmesbury, from the Waggon and Horses, every Thursday at Noon, for the Winter Season, and from the Royal Oak, at Tetbury, every Saturday at One o'Clock, proceeding directly for London, where he arrives at the King's-Arms Inn, Holbourn-Bridge, every Thursday morning; and sets out from thence early on Friday Morning, reaching Tetbury the Wednesday following at Noon, and Malmesbury, the Thursday at Noon.

N.B. Any Goods, in Haste for London, may be carried to Tetbury by One o'Clock on Saturdays, in the Winter Season.

Good Care will be taken, and constant Attendance given, to take in Goods, &c. at the King's-Arms Inn aforesaid, by Joseph Dutton, Master of the said Inn.

The said Thomas Shipton's other Waggons go to Wotton-Under-edge and Dursley, as usual, setting out from his own House, at Horsley, every Saturday Morning at Ten o'Clock, for the Winter Season, and calling at the Royal Oak, at Tetbury, at One o'Clock the same Day, where he takes in

Goods and Passengers, and proceeds directly to the King's-Head in the Old Change, London.

N.B. The above Malmesbury and Tetbury Waggons call at the White-Bear, in Piccadilly, going into, and coming out of London; and the Wotton-Underedge and Dursley Waggons, at the Black-Bear.

No Money, Bank Notes, Plate, Jewels, &c. will be insured, unless entered as such, and paid for accordingly.

Whoever favour me with their Carriage shall be well used, and their Goods taken great Care of.

119   *11 March 1765*

SALISBURY FAIR.

On the Thursday before the said Fair a Waggon will set out from Stroud, through Rodborough's Butts, Hampton, &c. for Salisbury. Gentlemen, Tradesmen, and others, who have any Goods to send, may depend upon the greatest Care by,

Their humble Servant,
D. BALLARD.

N.B. The constant Stage Waggon from Glocester to Bristol, through Painswick, Stroud, Hampton, and the Bottoms, Tetbury, Didmarton, Sodbury, &c. &c. continues as usual.

120   *19 July 1790*

Gloucester and Bristol Common Stage Waggons.

Thomas Gardiner respectfully informs his friends, and the public in general, that his Waggon sets out from the George Inn, Castle-street, Bristol, every Wednesday morning, through Sodbury, Tetbury, Hampton, Nailsworth, Horsley, Woodchester, Rooksmore, Rodborough, Dudbridge, Cainscross, Stonehouse, Stanley, Easington, Stroud, Chalford, Bisley, and Painswick, and meets the following waggons regularly every week at the warehouses on the Quay, Glocester, viz. Cheltenham, Worcester, Hereford, Monmouth, and Brecon, by which Goods are expeditiously conveyed.

Gardiner likewise forwards Goods to all parts of England, North and South Wales.

Goods are likewise forwarded from his Warehouse, the George Inn, Castle-street, Bristol, for Bath, all parts of Somersetshire, Devonshire, and the West of England.

121   *15 August 1791*

The Proprietors of the London, Cirencester, Stroudwater, and Tetbury Coaches, beg leave to inform Clothiers and others, who may, for the future, send Cloth, &c. by the above Coaches, that they will not be answerable for any damage it may sustain in carriage, in consequence of which, they have reduced the price to One Penny per pound; and as the damage frequently happens from bad package, the Proprietors request every person who may have occasion to send Cloth by the said Coaches, to have it well packed, and they will use every means in their power to prevent its receiving any injury, and deliver it with all expedition.

August 5, 1791.

122 *10 February 1794*

Rodborough, Feb. 5, 1794

Whereas on Monday evening last, between the hours of nine and ten o'clock, a Truss, packed in Spanish Bag, (consisting of ten pieces of Superfine Cassimeres, directed to *Messrs. John Tate, & Co. London*) was feloniously stolen from out of Mr. John Niblett's London Waggon, on its way to town, about half a mile one side of Cirencester, on the Hampton road – five of which pieces were afterwards found, (taken out of the said Truss) in the possession of one William Green, of Cirencester aforesaid, who is committed to prison to take his trial for the same – the other five are yet undiscovered . . . Whoever will discover the other offender or offenders, so that he or they may be convicted shall receive a Reward of Five Guineas by me,

JOHN NIBLETT.

N.B. An accomplice making a discovery, shall be intitled to the same Reward.

123 *27 June 1796*

DANIEL NIBLETT,
Of Rodborough, in the County of Glocester.

Respectfully informs his Friends and the Public, that he has taken to the Business of a
LONDON CARRIER,

for many years carried on by his late Father, John Niblett, deceased. He returns his hearty thanks for the countenance and support, which his said Father, in his life time, experienced, and hopes, by a faithful attention to Business, to merit a continuance of the same.

A Waggon will set out from his Warehouse, at the Bear-Inn, Rodborough aforesaid, every Monday precisely at twelve o'clock at noon, and arrive at the George-Inn, Snowhill, in London, every Friday morning; and returns to the Bear-Inn aforesaid every Thursday.

A Bye Waggon occasionally on Wednesdays.

GLOUCESTERSHIRE
FLYING WAGGONS TO LONDON.

SAMUEL TANNER begs to announce, that, for the better accomodation of the Woollen Trade of this County, he intends to start a FLYING WAGGON every Evening, at Seven o'Clock precisely, (Saturday excepted,) from his Warehouse at Rodborough, to arrive at his Warehouse, Grub-Street, London, in two days; the Goods to be delivered very early in the Morning of the third day. To commence on the 1st of May, 1814.

The principle upon which these Waggons are to be Horsed will ensure Regularity and Dispatch.

N.B. No Goods can be forwarded per Fly, that do not arrive at the Warehouse, Rodborough, by Six o'Clock in the Evening. Slow Waggons as usual.

Waggons will leave the following Places as under, viz. –

Long's Warehouse, Wotton-Underedge, Monday and Thursday, half-past Ten o'Clock.

George Inn, Nailsworth, ditto, ditto, Two.

Falcon Inn, Painswick, Tuesday and Friday, Twelve.

Golden Heart Inn, Stroud, ditto, ditto, Two.

Company's Arms Inn, Chalford, ditto, ditto, Two.

Lamb Inn, Dursley, Wednesday and Saturday, half-past Ten.

Crown Inn, Uley, ditto, ditto, One.

Eastington, ditto, ditto, Eleven.

Golden Cross Inn, Cainscross, ditto, ditto, Two.

To prevent delay, it is particularly requested that a note may be sent with all Goods intended to go by the Fly, stating the Weight and Address of such Goods; also, that the Waggons sent to collect Goods may not be detained at the Manufactories, otherwise it will be impossible to forward it the same Evening.

All Accounts must be settled quarterly without discount.

Road-House, near Minchinhampton, March 26, 1814.

The Lechlade Route

One route which at certain times during the 18th century was particularly busy with wagon traffic was that between Gloucester and Lechlade. The small Thames-side town, the gateway to central Gloucestershire from London and the south-east, was perhaps the place in the county which had an economy the most dependent on the transport of goods. Although during the 18th century the Gloucester to London traffic gradually deserted the road through Lechlade in favour of the more northerly road through Oxford, all the traffic from the clothmaking country (featured in the last section) and from the market towns of central Gloucestershire still came through Lechlade. Many goods, too, were brought to the town to be unloaded there and put into barges bound for London, for Lechlade was the highest point of the Thames navigation and had its wharves, warehouses and wharfingers.

Cheese was the commodity most regularly loaded into the Thames barges at Lechlade, but in time of war with France many other goods were carried across the Cotswolds from Gloucester or Tewkesbury. Iron, ironware, and earthenware from Shropshire, Birmingham and the Potteries, goods which in peacetime were sent down the Severn in the trows to Bristol to be transhipped into coasting vessels for London, were diverted to this inland route because of the danger posed to shipping in the English Channel by the French privateers. The outbreak of war was signalled by the appearance in the *Journal* of the advertisements of the carriers and wharfingers operating this service, often in fierce competition. Examples are given below from the time of the war of the Austrian Succession, the Seven Years war, and the war with the American colonies which France came into in 1781 (nos. 125–7). Some notices relating to Lechlade's cheese trade given here (nos. 128–9) date from shortly after the completion of the canal link from the Severn to the Thames at Lechlade in 1789, which made it possible for goods to make the whole of the journey across England by water during the Napoleonic Wars. Richard Ainge, who figures in two of the extracts below, was from one of the most successful families of wharfingers based at Lechlade. The remains of the wharf from which the Ainges traded can still be seen at the bottom of the garden of their attractive little house adjoining Lechlade churchyard (cf. *V.C.H. Glos.* vii. 109).

125 *10 April 1744*

NOTICE is hereby given to all Merchants,
Tradesmen, &c.

That Mess. Pasco and Gardiner have a very large and the most convenient Storehouse for housing all Sorts of Goods, without any Expence of halling from the River, there being a Crane to draw up any Weight of Goods from any Vessel on the River. Great Care will be taken both in receiving and delivering out of Goods, at a very reasonable Price; and, if required, they will convey, or cause them to be convey'd, to London by Land; or to Letchlade, to go from thence by Water; or to and from any other Parts of England. Whoever may have any Occasion for the receiving here, or conveying of Goods hence, please to direct to the above Persons, at the Sugar-house, Gloucester . . .

A Gloucester–London carrier's wagon passing the new Millbank Penitentiary, Westminster, c. 1828.

RICHARD AINGE,
of Letchlade, in the County of Gloucester,
GIVES NOTICE to all Gentlemen, Merchants,
Traders, &c.

That he intends to follow the Business of a Wharfinger, being now in Possession of a Warehouse in the said Town, proper for the Reception and Conveyance of Goods from thence to London; which was an Occupation wherein his late Grandfather and Father were engaged: And he humbly hopes, that such Gentlemen, &c. that were pleased to favour his Predecessors with the Care of Housing and Conveying their Goods, will be so kind as to continue the same to,

Their most obedient Servant,
RICHARD AINGE;

Upon whose Diligence and Fidelity they may depend for a punctual Compliance with their respective Instructions.

126 *21 February 1758*

Leachlade, Feb. 10.

Notice is hereby given to Merchants, Tradesmen,
and others,

That, after the First Day of March next ensuing, I will not receive from, or forward to, Glocester, any Goods but what may come from or be consigned to, Mr. William Coles, and Mrs. Mary Wood, Wharfingers, in Glocester, Flour, Grain, Cheese, and Butter, excepted.

ROBERT ANDERSON.

———————

Leachlade, Feb. 10.

Whereas this Conveyance is now attended with many Inconveniences, on account of the Number of Persons at Glocester undertaking to send Goods thereby; In order therefore to a more regular Method, This is to inform all whom it may concern, That, after the First Day of March next, I will not forward from, or send to Glocester, any Goods, (Cheese, Butter, Flour, and Grain, excepted) unless I receive the same from, or they are ordered to the Care of, Mr. William Coles, or Mrs. Mary Wood, established Wharfingers there.

RICHARD AINGE.

28 February 1758

Glocester, Feb. 25.

In perusing the Glocester Journal on Monday last I saw Two remarkable Advertisements inserted, one by Mr. Richard Ainge, and the other by Mr. Robert Anderson, as the only Wharfingers in Lechlade, both to the subsequent Purport, viz. 'That, after the 1st Day of March next ensuing, they will not receive from, or forward to, Glocester, any Goods unless they come from, or are consigned to, Mr. William Coles, or Mrs. Mary Wood, Flour, Grain, Cheese, and Butter, only excepted:' In order to defeat such a monopolizing, monstrous, designing, and cruel Scheme, which would be a great Imposition on the Publick if not prevented, and is more particularly intended to prejudice me, I can with Pleasure inform all Merchants, Tradesmen, and others, That I have appointed an Agent, taken a commodious Wharf in Lechlade, have Waggons and Vessels enough to convey any Quantity of Goods from and to Glocester, Lechlade, Oxford, Abingdon, London, &c. &c. full as expeditious, and as reasonable as Mr. Coles, or Mrs. Wood: Instead of *Compelling*, I humbly intreat, the Continuance of their Favours whom I have served, and think myself much obliged to them; and those that I have not, may be assured no Care shall be wanting to expedite safely what Goods shall be consigned to

Their most humble Servant,
W. RUDGE.
Ironmonger and Wharfinger.

Query, whether or not they would have enhanced the Carriage if they had succeeded in their Scheme?

127 *9 July 1781*

To Merchants, Factors, and the Publick in general.

Permit me most respectfully to inform you, that I have taken and entered upon all that commodious Dwelling House, together with very spacious and extensive Warehouses and Wharfs thereunto belonging (the Property of Sir Jacob Wheate, Bart.) situate at the West Entrance of the Town of Lechlade, in the County of Glocester, which are now open for the Reception of all Sorts of Goods and Merchandizes consigned to and from London: And that for the greater Regularity and Dispatch of Business, a compact Stage Waggon, with strong and able Horses, will begin on Monday the 9th of July next, and continue every succeeding Week to go from Lechlade to Hereford, through Fairford, Cirencester, Glocester, and Ross, which will arrive early on Wednesday, and return early on Saturday following to Lechlade.

It may not be improper to observe, that some trifling Misunderstanding has of late subsisted between the Proprietors of the Wharfs at this Place, and much impeded the great Business that otherwise might have been done here, and for which this Place is most eligibly adapted; that all Differences are now amicably adjusted on the permanent Basis of Friendship, Unanimity, and mutual Interest; and that every Exertion will be made in order to carry on Business in the most extensive Manner, so as to merit the Approbation and Encouragement of the Publick.

Lechlade, June 25, 1781   W. SIRRELL.

N.B. All Goods, &c. brought by this Waggon from Hereford to Lechlade, will be received free from any Expence for Wharfage or Warehouse-Room.

HENRY BURDEN, Wharfinger,
And Agent to the Cheesemongers of London, at
their Warehouse, Buscott, Berks, and at
Leachlade, Glocestershire,

Most respectfully informs his Friends and the public in general, that the navigation between the two capitals, London and Bristol, is now open, by the Thames and Severn Canal, for the passage of boats. All goods consigned to him, will be forwarded with care and dispatch. Vessels are ready to take in goods weekly, or oftener if required, for London and Bristol, Cirencester, Stroud, Glocester, Worcester, Shrewsbury, and all places adjacent to the Canal and river Severn, which has its union with the Liverpool and Birmingham canals at Stourport.

N.B. As soon as the sundry freights and charges can be ascertained to the different places, the public may depend on the earliest information. His connections are, Mr. Benjamin Winckworth, wharfinger, Queenhithe, London; Mr. Benjamin Grazebrook, of Stroud, whose vessels go regularly every Spring to, and return from Bristol; Mr. John Coles, and Mrs. Mary Kellow, wharfingers, Glocester; to whom all goods consigned will meet a regular dispatch.

TO CHEESE FACTORS.
Glocester.

Rowland Heane, London Carrier, impressed with a grateful sense of past favors, begs leave to present his sincere acknowledgements; and respectfully informs the Public in general, and Factors (sending their Cheese down the Severn) in particular, that all Goods consigned to his care, will be forwarded to London, or the intermediate places, with all possible expedition, either by his Waggons (which set out from Glocester three times a week) or by the way of Letchlade without any charges or expences whatever, for wharfage, housage, &c. And having engaged large and convenient warehouses, for the purpose of stowing Cheese, he flatters himself Factors will find a considerable advantage in consigning their goods to him, as beside the utmost attention to care and dispatch, they will make a saving of two shillings and sixpence per ton, which it has been customary to charge for Wharfage, &c.

The Carriers and the Turnpikes

The carriers were the road-users who most often found themselves in dispute with the road authorities of the day, the turnpike trusts. The trusts secured statutory powers to enforce various measures that were

A timber wagon in Tewkesbury, c. 1835.

designed to cut down the wear and tear caused to their roads by the carriers' heavy wagons. Tolls were made to relate to the weight of the loads carried; the number of horses that could be used was restricted, as a method of cutting down the size of the loads; and a minimum size was laid down for the width of the rims of the wagons' wheels, broader wheels being thought to do less damage to the road surface. The question of the size of the wheels gave rise to considerable debate, some of it of a technical nature (no. 132); and the restrictions as a whole were naturally resented by the local waggoners and long-distance carriers, whose operating costs, in which turnpike tolls were in any case a major item, were much increased. Methods of evading the higher tolls were commonly resorted to, and the resentment sometimes took the form of open violence against the toll-collectors (nos. 131, 136).

Enforcing tolls by weight on the carriers involved the turnpike trusts in the provision of weighing-machines at some of their tollgates. One was installed at the gate near Over bridge in 1755 (*G.J.* 15 July); and by the early years of the 19th century the work of installing and maintaining machines for the local trusts was sufficient to support at least one Gloucester business, that of William Jarrett (no. 138; and see Glos. R.O., D 204/1/2 (29 Jan. 1800); D 204/3/2 (17 Oct. 1805)).

130 *16 July 1745*

> The Trustees, appointed in and by an Act of Parliament, intitled, An Act for continuing, and making more effectual, an Act made in the 9th Year of the Reign of his late Majesty King George the First, for repairing the Highways from the City of Gloucester to the Top of Birdlip-Hill, (being the Road to London) and from the Foot of the said Hill to the Top of Crickley Hill, (being the Road to Oxford) do hereby give Notice, That if any Person or Persons (whether travelling for Hire, or not for Hire) shall, after the first Day of August next, travel on any Part of the Roads, directed to be repaired by the said Acts, with any Carriage drawn by more than six Horses, such Person or Persons will be dealt with as the Law directs.

131 *25 August 1766*

> Whereas I, the underwritten John Long, of Kilcot, in the Parish of Hawkesbury, in the County of Gloucester, Labourer, did some Time since assault and beat John King, the Toll-taker at the Turnpike between Wortley and Wotton-Underedge, in the said County, for refusing to let me pass the said Turnpike with a Waggon Toll free, for which a Prosecution was thereupon commenced against me by the said John King, under the Direction of the Trustees of the said Turnpike, but upon making the said John King Satisfaction for the Injury done him, acknowledging my Offence

in the Glocester Journal, and Promise of good Behaviour for the future, such Prosecution is to be dropped: Now I do hereby acknowledge That I was guilty of a very great Offence, as well against the Public as the said John King, in assaulting and beating him as above mentioned; and I do hereby ask his Pardon for so doing, and promise for the future not to offend in like Manner again.

Witness my Hand the 28th of July,

Witness JOHN WALSH.   JOHN LONG.

132 *30 November 1767*

To The
Printer of the GLOCESTER JOURNAL.

Mr. Raikes,

As there is a probability that many amendments will be made in the act passed last session for the preservation of the highways, I beg leave, by means of your useful Paper, to submit to the consideration of the Members of the Hon. House of Commons, and to the public, the following construction of a waggon, which, in the opinion of several Commissioners of the Turnpikes, and many eminent Wheelwrights, is better calculated for preserving the roads, and more useful, than any of the broad-wheeled waggons now in use.

I am Sir,
Your humble servant,
Notgrove, Glocestershire,   WILLIAM WOOD.
Nov. 28.

The wheels in breadth are about six inches and a quarter; the fore wheels going from out to out about six feet two inches; the hind wheels from inside to inside four feet asunder; the bed is four feet in the clear in the narrowest part, being wrathed and bowed in the hill-country fashion; and by putting on a top-wrathe and hoops, it may be, and has been, made a very convenient tilted waggon; these may be taken off or put on as occasion requires. The wheels going plain, by their play beats a track about 13 or 14 inches wide; and the horses drawing in pairs, this track is found a very good width to travel in. This waggon is very convenient in home business, as it does not cut the ground in carrying hay, corn, &c. and as the wheels may be taken off for dung carts. It has been used upwards of two years, and by experience is found very serviceable in doing a great deal of business. In going on the coach road, where no other double waggon goes, it keeps the quarters very plain, whereas the track of the common nine-inch wheels is not wide enough for a horse to work in. The wheelwrights say, they can make these carriages almost as light as the three-inch ones, only in the rim of the wheel; whereas in the nine-inch wheel they must make it very heavy, or it will contain no strength, as it lies so wide from the bear of the spoke. These six-inch wheels are so strong in their make, that they would carry vast weights, therefore it would be proper to allow, with the carriage included, only five tons as a sufficient load. This carriage has travelled the Glocester, Tewkesbury, and Evesham roads for two years past, without any interruption, drawing eight horses; but being disabled from so doing by the letter of the said act, the proprietor humbly hopes, with a great number of his brother farmers, that the Legislature will take into consideration the expediency of allowing them such a carriage, the conveniences of which are so obvious.

133 *18 October 1773*

Notice is hereby given, that all Persons passing through the Eastgate Turnpike with narrow Wheel Waggons, Carts, &c. that are of a lesser Breadth or Gage than six Inches, are to pay, from the 31st Instant, one Half Toll more than they usually have paid, except Teams employed in Husbandry only. By Order of the Commissioners,

JOHN NICHOLAS, Clerk.

N.B. No Pair of Wheels shall be wider than four Feet six Inches from Inside to Inside, to be measured at the Ground.

134 *3 January 1774*

WEIGHING ENGINES,

For Weighing Carriages on Turnpike Roads with Ease, Dispatch, and Accuracy, are made and erected by JAMES EDGELL, of Frome, Somerset. These Engines are of a new Construction, and may be placed where those of the old Construction cannot, a Space of Ground of 15 Feet Square, and four Feet in Depth, being sufficient for erecting one of these. They will weigh from one Pound to nine Tons and upwards, and the Weight used for weighing each Ton is only 14 Pounds. The Scale hangs above Ground in the most convenient Part of the Turnpike or Weighing House, and a Quarter Guinea will turn the Beam. By these Engines a small Parcel of Goods as well as a loaded Carriage may be weighed with Accuracy; and a loaded Carriage is weighed with as much Ease and Expedition as a small Parcel in common Scales.

Engines of this Construction are erected at the City of Bristol.

135 *1 April 1776*

To the Commissioners of the Turnpike Roads between the Cities of Hereford and Glocester.

Public Notice is hereby given, that Thomas Yeates, London-Carrier, intends, upon the 29th of May next, to draw Waggons with 16 inch Wheels, in Pursuance of the Statute in that Case made and provided. It is therefore expected, that the said Commissioners do cause the Turnpike Road between the said Cities of Hereford and Glocester to be made of a sufficient Breadth to permit the said Waggons to pass, or otherwise he will lay Information against the several Parishes where any Obstruction shall be found, as Witness my Hand this 1st Day of April, 1776,

THOMAS YEATES.

136 *8 December 1783*

Northgate Turnpike near Glocester.

Whereas Information hath been given, That several Carriers have lately made it a Practice to unload Goods, Wares, and Merchandizes, from Carts, Waggons, and other Carriages, at certain Houses adjoining to this Road, before the same Carts, Waggons, and other Carriages, come to the Weighing Engine erected at this Turnpike in Pursuance of the Act of Parliament; and also that several Carriers make it a Practice to send Goods from Glocester beyond the Weighing Machine, to be lodged in the said Houses until the Waggons and other Carriages come along, and then load the same, in order to defraud the Pike; and that several Persons, travelling the said Road with Carriages, have caused the Soles of the Wheels to be made round instead of being made flat, whereby the Road is much injured and cut; Notice is hereby given, That if, after this Publication, any Person shall be detected in any of the Offences aforesaid, he will be prosecuted as the Act of Parliament directs,

Glocester, Dec. 6.

By Order of the Trustees,
H. WILTON, Clerk.

137 *7 October 1811*

On Wednesday last, the proprietors and driver of a common stage-wagon were severally convicted, . . . the former in the penalty of 5*l.* and the latter in the penalty of 20*s.* for driving the said waggon on the turnpike-road, between Tewkesbury and Gloucester, with a greater number of horses than are allowed by the general turnpike-act. The proprietors were also convicted in the mitigated penalty of 20*s.* for not having their names, places of abode, and description of the waggon, painted upon *a conspicuous part thereof,* as required by the said act.

138 *28 October 1811*

To the Gentlemen Commissioners of his Majesty's
Turnpike-Roads

SAMUEL ULETT,
WEIGHING MACHINE MAKER & WHITESMITH,
(Formerly Apprentice to the late Wm. Jarrett, deceased,)

Begs leave to inform the Gentlemen Commissioners of his Majesty's Turnpikes, &c. that having assisted his late Master W.J. in making and erecting Weighing Machines, and since made the construction of them a

94

principal part of his Study, flatters himself he is perfect Master of the Business in all its Branches, and therefore humbly offers himself to their Notice.

N.B. Weighing Machines carefully erected and adjusted, Old ones repaired. – New Inn Lane, Gloucester, Oct. 26, 1811.

CHAPTER FIVE

Travellers

This chapter is a miscellany, the intention being to give an impressionistic view of the many and varied types of traveller, for whom the road, and its inns, low lodging-houses, or wayside camping-places, was a way of life. The first group might be described as the legitimate businessmen; the second group comprises the disreputable or unashamedly dishonest travelling folk; and the third group includes the travelling showmen and entertainers.

Tradesmen and Others

The most numerous category in this group was probably that made up of the common pedlars or hawkers, providers of a variety of small goods on their rounds of isolated villages or from their pitches at fairs. It would be interesting to know how successful was the licensing system by which the authorities attempted to control and keep track of them (no. 149); in 1683 it was recorded that numerous Scots pedlars operating within Wiltshire were using Tetbury, just across the county boundary as their base, making it easier for them to avoid the attentions of the county magistrates (*Calendar of State Papers, Domestic*, xxvi. 83-4). Besides the pedlars many poor men of various trades were to be found on the roads, among them itinerant basket-makers, thatchers, hedgers, and, at harvest time, gangs of reapers; the notice inserted before the harvest in 1759 (no. 140) shows the dependence of local farms on a seasonal influx of migratory labour, and the scale of that influx is indicated by a report in 1773 (*G.J.* 16 Aug.) which mentions that more than 140 reapers were at work on one large farm at Churcham, near Gloucester. The poor tradesmen and farmworkers who tramped the roads did not of course advertise in the papers for work but found it by calling at farmhouses or by taking their stand at one of the hiring fairs that were held once or twice a year in the larger market towns, and so references to such people in the *Journal* are sparse and mainly incidental. Some idea of the variety of ways in which a living could be made on the road is provided by the extracts in the next section, where will be found amongst others a man who had been employed as a groom to take a stud horse about the countryside on its various engagements, an absconded shoemaker who was thought to be picking up a living on his way to the coast by his trade and by casual harvest-work, and a 'strolling rat-catcher'.

In a different class were the more substantial tradesmen and shopkeepers who travelled regularly to find their customers at markets and fairs. Examples are provided by the Cirencester whipmaker (no. 139), the first part of whose advertisement refers to the great sheep-fair held at Weyhill in Hampshire; by the Painswick goldsmith (no. 143); and by a 'travelling linen-draper' whose death in a road accident was reported in 1808 (*G.J.* 21 Nov.). Probably rather more exceptional was the enterprising Henry Whittick of Gloucester, one of the *Journal's* most regular advertisers, who dogged the footsteps of the fashionable at race-meetings and other social events, selling everything from perfumes to fire-arms (nos. 146, 152). Others whose movements were to some extent dictated by those of fashionable society were the more successful of the travelling medical men and the hairdresser in no. 145, whose advertisement is one of six placed in the same issue by hairdressers from Bath and London who were in Gloucester for the Three Choirs festival.

The commercial traveller, employed by the larger businesses, was already a familiar figure on the road by the end of the 18th century. The advertisers in nos. 148 and 154, seeking employment by the Gloucester-shire clothiers, appear to have been at the top of their line of business; a more usual type was perhaps represented by 'a genteel, well-made Man, who said he belonged to a Warehouse in Birmingham' who left a horse at a Gloucester inn in 1758 (*G.J.* 28 March). By the beginning of the 19th century the 'commercial gentlemen' had their regular haunts among the inns (nos. 151, 153) and perhaps had already developed those particular conventions that Trollope described so well in his account of Mr Moulder and his companions at the Leeds inn in Chapter Six of *Orley Farm*.

One group of regular travellers who made occasional appearances in the *Journal's* columns were its own newsmen (no. 150), who formed the complex distribution network that enabled the paper to boast in 1735 (23 Dec.) that it 'is extended the farthest of any in England by special Messengers.' A few years later Raikes put out an advertisement that listed 21 'divisions' or rounds by which his paper was carried as far afield as Carmarthen, Taunton, Salisbury, and Stourbridge (Glouc. Library, Glos. Colln. NV 26.1).

139 *3 September 1734*

Tho. Blackwell, of Cirencester,

Will be at Way-Hill, during the whole Fair next Michaelmas, with all Sorts of Hand-Whips, by what Name soever call'd, both Men's and Women's; where any Dealers may be serv'd at the lowest Prices. N.B. He is the Maker.

He also will have with him, all Sorts of Whip-Thongs, and Choice of Silk Lashes, and Whip-cord; Red and Tann'd Bazils, Shokes for canvassing of Saddle-Trees, and Pannelling-Cloth; with many other Sorts of Goods in the Saddler's Way.

Any old Whips, if not too far worn, Handle and Buttons good, may be made up again as neat, as if new.

He stands in the Webb-Row, near the Salisbury Cutlers.

He likewise intends to keep the two Fairs at Stow, viz. that on the 13th of October next, and the First of May following, with the same Sorts of Goods.

He also sells many Sorts of Shoemakers Leather, with Incle and Spinnal, Masheen, and Black Balls.

And he keeps a Mercer's Shop in the Market-place in Cirencester; where are sold, at the lowest Prices, all sorts of Mercery and Funeral Goods.

140 *3 July 1759*

Whereas it is the Complaint of a Number of Gentlemen in this City and Parts adjacent, That there is great Want of Hands to get in the Harvest, occasioned by an Apprehension in the laborious Part of the Inland Country, that if they come near Glocester they will be impressed by me into the Sea-Service; These are to certify all such who may be concerned herein, That no Landmen have been impressed by me, or the Officers under my Direction, since my Residence here; And I do hereby further declare, That no Landmen shall be impressed by my Officers, but that all such as may come here may follow their different Occupations in Safety.

Given under my Hand, in the City of Glocester, the 28th Day of June, 1759.

WM. BROWNE.

141 *4 August 1761*

On Saturday Evening last the Chevalier Taylor returned to this City from Hereford, where he was attended by an extraordinary Concourse of Persons afflicted in the Eye, on account of his happy Success with those who passed under his Care in his First Passage. The Chevalier, from various Invitations, is obliged to proceed hence, on his Return to his House in Leicester Fields, in the following Order: He left this City last Night and is now at Ledbury, will be this Evening at the Unicorn in Leominster, To-morrow Evening at the Post-House in Ludlow, on Wednesday Evening at the Crown in Worcester, on Friday Evening at Banbury, and on Saturday Evening next, the 8th Instant, at the Star in Oxford; where, after giving some Lectures as usual in the Art of restoring Sight, he will continue his Road for London. Agreeable to an exact List of those who have been under his Care in his Tour thro' Wales, they appear to have exceeded 500 different Persons, amongst whom are many of the greatest Note in those Provinces.

142 *3 January 1780*

GLOCESTER.

George Roth, Portrait Painter, is arrived here from Bristol, who takes likenesses in Miniature in Oil Colours, at so low a Price as 25s. Picture and Frame. Specimens of many likenesses done in Glocester may be seen at his Lodgings at Mrs. Hill's, in the Southgate-Street.

143 *4 September 1780*

PAINSWICK, Glocestershire

Richard Land, Goldsmith, begs Leave to inform his Friends, and the Public in general, that he has lately declined keeping Markets and Fairs, (and returns his sincere Thanks for the many Encouragements they have been pleased to give him) but carries on Business at his Shop as usual, and sells all Kinds of Plate, Rings, Watches, plated Buckles and Spurs, and every other Article in that Branch on the Lowest Terms; and executes Orders with the greatest Exactness, and utmost Expedition.

N.B. Ready Money for old Gold and Silver. Mourning Rings at the shortest Notice.

144 *12 July 1784*

Mr. Joseph, the celebrated and famous Corn-Cutter, from Bath, most respectfully acquaints the Ladies and Gentlemen of Glocester, and its vicinity, that he is just arrived here . . .

145 *6 September 1784*

TO THE LADIES.

Howell, Hair-Dresser, from Bath, begs leave to inform the nobility and gentry that he intends being at Glocester during the Music-Meeting. To be heard of at the Lower-George, Westgate-street.

Those ladies, who will please to honour him with their commands, by giving timely notice, may depend upon being waited on with the strictest punctuality.

146 *18 July 1785*

GLOCESTER

Whittick, Hair-Dresser and Perfumer, opposite the Boothall, in the Westgate Street, returns his most grateful thanks for the generous

Advertisement.

WHEREAS *R. RAIKES* hath with great Labour and Expence Eſtabliſh'd a PRINTING-OFFICE in the City of GLOUCESTER, from whence is Publiſh'd, every Week, A NEWS-PAPER, call'd, *THE GLOUCESTER JOURNAL*, which hath met with great Encouragement from the Publick, it being of far greater Advantage for Advertiſing of Buſineſs, than any other News-Paper on this Side the Country, by reaſon of the Number of Men employ'd in diſperſing it in the ſeveral Counties herein mentioned : In order therefore to make the ſaid JOURNAL ſtill more Uſeful, the Printer thereof hath ſettled Correſpondents in the Cities of *Briſtol, Saliſbury, Worceſter* and *Hereford*, alſo in the Town of *Taunton*, and other Places, whereby Perſons may have their Buſineſs tranſmitted to the ſaid Printing-Office, and diſpatch'd as expeditiouſly as can be deſired : And farther, to make this Paper yet more Univerſal, and render it Pleaſant as well as Profitable, we ſhall always endeavour (in the Dearth of News) to divert our Readers with ſomething New and Entertaining.——For the Satisfaction of thoſe that are willing to encourage this ſo Uſeful a Work, and that they may be fully ſatisfy'd their Buſineſs will be carefully per-form'd, there is hereunto annex'd a LIST of the Names of the Men who diſtribute the ſaid JOURNAL, with the Names of the Cities and Principal Towns, in each County, of their reſpective Diviſions.

Firſt Diviſion.
JOHN FLOWER, *Diſtributer to the City of* Gloucester.

Second Diviſion.
REBECCA EVANS, *Book-ſeller, on St. James's*-Back, Briſtol, *and her Agents, Diſtributers to the City of* Briſtol.

Third Diviſion.
WILLIAM NORRIS, *Book-ſeller in* Taunton, *and his Agents, Diſtributers to*
Taunton, *Somerſetſhire*
Bridgewater, *ditto*
Dunſter, *ditto*
Minehead, *ditto*
Wellington, *ditto, &c.*

Fourth Diviſion.
JOHN PEWTRIS, *Diſtributer.*
Stroudwater, *Gloucestershire*
Minchinhampton, *ditto*
Tedbury, *ditto*
Malmesbury, *Wilts*
Chippenham, *ditto*
Calne, *ditto*
Devizes, *ditto, &c.*

Fifth Diviſion.
THOMAS OVENS, *Diſtributer.*
Sean, *Wilts*
Weſtbury, *ditto*
Warminſter, *ditto*
Hindon, *ditto*
Maiden-Bradley, *ditto*
Wincaunton, *Somerſetſhire, &c.*

Sixth Diviſion.
SAMUEL PINCOTT, *Diſtributer.*
Marſhfield, *Gloucestershire*
Bath, *Somerſetſhire, &c.*

Seventh Diviſion.
THOMAS PREEN, *Diſtributer.*
Stonehouſe, *Gloucestershire*
Stanley, *ditto*
Nimphsfield, *ditto*
Sherſton, *Wilts*
Corſham, *ditto*
Bradford, *ditto*
Trowbridge, *ditto, &c.*

Eighth Diviſion.
JOHN SMITH, *Diſtributer.*
Philips-Norton, *Somerſetſhire*
Froom, *ditto*
Shepton-Mallet, *ditto*
Wells, *ditto*
Glaſtenbury, *ditto*
Bruton, *ditto, &c.*

Ninth Diviſion.
SAMUEL BEARD, *Diſtributer.*
Painſwick, *Gloucestershire*
Biſley, *ditto*
Cirenceſter, *ditto*
Fairford, *ditto*
Letchlade, *ditto*
Highworth, *Wilts*
Swinden, *ditto*
Marlborough, *ditto*
Wootton-Baſſet, *ditto, &c.*

Tenth Diviſion.
HENRY ROOK, *Diſtributer.*
Cheltenham, *Gloucestershire*
Winchcombe, *ditto*
Campden, *ditto*
Eveſham, *Worceſterſhire*
Parſhore, *ditto, &c.*

Eleventh Diviſion.
THOMAS ROOK, *Diſtributer.*
Northleach, *Gloucestershire*
Burford, *Oxfordſhire*
Whitney, *ditto*
Bampton o' th' Buſh, *ditto*
Farringdon. *Berkſhire*
Stanford, *ditto*
Wantage, *ditto*
Stow o' th' Wold, *Gloucestershire*
Moreton-in-Marſh, *ditto, &c.*

Twelfth Diviſion.
WILLIAM OAKEY, *Diſtributer.*
Tewkſbury, *Gloucestershire*
Upton upon Severn, *Worceſterſhire*
Worceſter
Bewdley, *ditto*
Kidderminſter, *ditto*
Stourbridge, *Worceſterſhire*
Bromſgrove, *ditto*
Droitwich, *ditto, &c.*

Thirteenth Diviſion.
JAMES NOTT, *Diſtributer.*
Mitchel-Dean, *Gloucestershire*
Roſs, *Herefordſhire*
Hereford, *&c.*

Fourteenth Diviſion.
THOMAS TIDMAN, *Diſtributer.*
Frampton, *Gloucestershire*
Cambridge-Inn, *ditto*
Durſley, *ditto*
Wootton-Underedge, *ditto*
Wickwar, *ditto*
Chipping-Sodbury, *ditto*
Thornbury, *ditto*
Berkeley, *ditto, &c.*

Fifteenth Diviſion.
THO. MAVERLY, *Diſtributer.*
Newnham, *Gloucestershire*
Lidney, *ditto*
Chepſtow, *Monmouthſhire*
Newport, *ditto*
Cardiffe, *Glamorganſhire*
Llandaff, *ditto, &c.*

Sixteenth Diviſion.
JA. SALCOMBE, *Diſtributer.*
Little-Dean, *Gloucestershire*
Coleford, *ditto*
Monmouth
Abergavenny, *Monmouthſhire*
Pont y Pool, *ditto*
Uſk, *ditto, &c.*

Seventeenth Diviſion.
THO. LEWIS, *Diſtributer.*
Newent, *Gloucestershire*
Ledbury, *Herefordſhire*
Bromyard, *ditto*
Tenbury, *Worceſterſhire*
Leominſter, *Herefordſhire*
Ludlow, *Shropſhire, &c.*

Eighteenth Diviſion.
WM. BROSSIER, *Diſtributer.*
Weſt-Lavington, *Wilts*
Market-Lavington, *ditto*
Shrewton, *ditto*
Stoke, *ditto*
Newton, *ditto*
Salisbury, *ditto*
Netherhaven, *ditto*
Uphaven, *ditto*
Charlton, *ditto, &c.*

Nineteenth Diviſion.
Rd. WILLIAMS, *Diſtributer.*
Hay, *Brecknockſhire*
Brecknock
Trecaſtle, *Brecknockſhire*
Lanimdovery, *Carmarthenſhire*
Langadock, *ditto*
Carmarthen, *&c.*

Twentieth Diviſion.——BRAYNE VAUGHAN, Diſtributer to *Weobley, Hearſley, Kington, Preſteign, Knighton, Clunn, Biſhop's-Caſtle, Shrewsbury, Welſhpool,* and *Newtown.*——N. B. *The two laſt Diviſions were made for the Conveniency of the Gentlemen and Tradeſmen of* Hereford, *&c.*

Twenty-firſt Diviſion.——RICHARD MAYO, Diſtributer to *Witney, Kingſton, Abingdon, Oxford,* and *Woodſtock.*

Advertisement by Robert Raikes the elder for the *Gloucester Journal*, listing his distributors, *c.* 1738.

encouragement he has been honoured with in business, and most respectfully solicits a continuance of support. He has just received from the first shops in London the choicest English and foreign perfumes, essences, eaux, pomades, and powders, at the very lowest prices . . .

Whittick intends being at Cowbridge on Tuesday the 19th inst. being the day preceding the races, and may be heard of at the Green Dragon. He begs leave to inform the Nobility and Gentry, that he has with him Figaro curls and cushions, dress chignons, carnation powder, which never soils the cloaths, and every article to compleat a Lady's head dress in the genteelest and most elegant fashion.

Whittick intends being at Worcester Music-Meeting, and Cirencester Races. He may be heard of at Worcester at Mr. William's, hair-dresser, High-street; and at Cirencester at the White-Hart.

147 *11 May 1789*

Mr. Moor, Surgeon Dentist, from Oxford, will attend this day, the 11th instant, at the George, in Stroud, for all operations in the Teeth and Gums, particularly for setting artificial (*sic*), transplanting and ingrafting human Teeth on the old stumps, till Thursday the 14th instant.

148 *15 November 1790*

TO MERCHANTS.

A Person, well-acquainted with Ireland, and who has travelled there for some time, under an engagement of procuring orders on commission for different houses in the Yorkshire worsted and woollen branches, would be glad to engage on a similar plan, with any respectable house in the superfine broad cloth, and fancy waistcoat line. He is a native of Yorkshire, has his general residence in Dublin, and can produce satisfactory testimonials of his abilities and integrity from his present employers.

Letters addressed to J.L. to be left with the printer, will be duly attended to.

149 *24 July 1797*

TO HAWKERS AND PEDLARS

Licences will be granted by applying at the following places, viz . . .

Persons offending against the Laws are liable to the following penalties: Not having the words *Licensed Hawkers*, together with the number, name, or other mark or marks of distinction written, printed, or painted upon the most conspicuous part of every Bag, Pack, Box, Cart, &c. Ten Pounds.

Unlicensed Persons so marking Packs, &c. Ten Pounds.

Persons found trading without Licence, contrary to the Act, Ten Pounds, one half to his Majesty, and the other to the Informer.

Any person whatsoever may lawfully seize and detain an Hawker, in order to give notice to a Constable, or other Peace Officer or Officers, who are required by the Act to carry such person before a Magistrate, unless he shall in the mean time produce his Licence; and in case of refusal or neglect each and every such Officer or Officers shall forfeit for each offence the sum of Ten Pounds.
July 10, 1797

150 *5 January 1807*

On Thursday died, at Bristol, aged 70, Mr. John Price, of this city, distributor of this Paper in the vicinity of Bristol, upwards of 30 years. He was extremely unwell when he left his house on the preceding Saturday; but no entreaty could prevail in dissuading him from setting off, as usual, to walk to Bristol, which, from extreme illness, he did not reach till Tuesday, and died two days afterwards. He was a man of strict integrity, and amassed considerable property in the unremitting discharge of his laborious duty. [Any temporary disappointment which our Readers may have experienced in the above district, will naturally be imputed to the loss of their faithful old Newsman]

151 . *7 December 1807*

GLOUCESTER
LOWER GEORGE INN AND TRAVELLERS'
HOTEL.
R. RIDLER,

Impresssed with the most lively sense of gratitude for the past favours conferred on him, most respectfully begs leave to solicit a continuance of Public Patronage; and assures those who may honour him with their favours, that no exertions shall be wanting, on his part, to merit their good opinion and recommendation. The utmost assiduity shall be manifested to render the abode of GENTLEMEN TRAVELLERS commodious and comfortable; and he trusts, by sedulous attention, to merit for his House, the enviable distinction of "THE TRAVELLERS' HOME."

Comfortable Sitting-rooms; light and warm Bedchambers. The Larder constantly well supplied. The Cellars well stored. Stabling, equal to any in the Kingdom. Hay and Corn, of the best qualities.

London and Provincial Newspapers.

152 *15 June 1807*

Whittick is at Bibury.

H. Whittick begs leave to inform the Nobility and Gentry, in the vicinity of Glocester, and Cheltenham, for their accomodation, he has Opened an Elegant Magazine, near the Church, Cheltenham, where Ladies and Gentlemen may be supplied with Articles of the newest Fashion, on the lowest terms; viz.–

An elegant Assortment of Jewellery . . . (*lists jewellery, perfumes, razors, braces, umbrellas, etc.*)

Whittick intends being at the following Races, Watering, and Bathing Places, during the Summer Season, as usual; and may be heard of at the Lamb Inn, Northleach, June 15th, and during the Bibury Race Week: Whittick intends being at Cardiff, (at Mr. Bird's,) on Monday, June 22d, and during the Race Week, Wednesday, Thursday, and Friday; will attend at Swansea, Carmarthen, Haverfordwest, Pembroke, and Tenby – may be heard of at Mr Haile's, White Lion, Tenby; at Mr. Dorchester's, Nag's Head, Hereford, during the Music Meeting; and at Hunter's Hall, during the Race Week, at Kingscote . . .

19 September 1808

WHITTICK *is at* KINGSCOTE!

Whittick most respectfully acquaints his numerous Friends and kind Patrons, that he will attend at Hunter's Hall, during the Meeting; and will think himself honoured in being favoured with their commands. Whittick will have with him, one of the best Single-barrel Guns in the kingdom; and has for Sale, excellent Double and Single-barrel Guns and Pistols, a Brace of Staunch Pointers, a Brace of capital Greyhounds, of the Snowball Breed, and a beautiful Couple of Cocking Spaniels, bred by Lord Sherborne.

153 *22 May 1820*

LAMB INN,
OPPOSITE BETTISON's LIBRARY,
HIGH-STREET, CHELTENHM.
JOHN GOMM

Begs leave to return his sincere Thanks to those Friends who have honoured him with their Support since he entered upon the above Inn . . .

J.G. begs to intimate to Commercial Gentlemen, that he has, at considerable expence, fitted up a separate part of his Establishment entirely for their reception, and humbly hopes by invariable attention to their accomodation and comfort, to merit a share of their Patronage. The Lamb Inn is situate in the most central and improving part of the High-Street, and in a direct line of Road to Chester, Holyhead, and all parts of the North . . .

154 *7 January 1822*

A Traveller, who has a connexion with the Woollen Drapers through the Northern and Midland Counties, which he has regularly visited for the last Ten years, is desirous to represent any respectable Clothing House, either by Commission or otherwise. The most respectable references will be given. Adress W.E. Post-Office, Shrewsbury.

In this group the gypsy is the figure that will need the least introduction. The two extracts (nos. 155, 172) show him as an amoral, lawless figure, an object of curiosity to settled eyes but softened by none of the romantic aura with which later writers were to invest him. Two other groups who appear to have been regarded in much the same light as the gypsies, though brought into the county by more legitimate business, were the Welsh drovers and the navvies. The drovers were a familiar sight on the minor roads and green lanes of Gloucestershire, herding their black cattle through the Vale and over the Cotswolds towards the fattening grounds in the Home Counties. The Gloucester innkeeper whose advertisement is quoted above (Chapter II no. 27) evidently welcomed their custom as they passed through the city, but that they had an unsavoury reputation at a later date is suggested by the account of a highway robbery near Bristol in 1807 (*G.J.* 1 June) when the victim was reported to have described his attacker as 'an ill-looking fellow . . . having the appearance of a Welch drover'. The account book of a rector of Barnsley, a village on one of the drovers' main routes, the Welsh Way, contains a record of their regular overnight stops in the village during the 1770s, when they paid him for the use of a field (Glos. R.O., D 269B/F 13); but it is likely that they were not always so scrupulous about seeking permission from the landowners along the way before turning their cattle into pasture, and the night-time incident referred to in no. 171 presumably resulted from some such cause. The navvies were a class of labourer which appeared on the roads increasingly as the 18th century advanced, travelling to jobs on the new canals and turnpike roads that were being built. The men responsible for the trouble at a Cainscross inn in 1779 had presumably moved, with their bulldog, down to the Stroudwater canal from a job on the Stourbridge canal which was under construction at the same time (no. 161; Thomas Cosham was landlord of the White Horse at Cainscross: Glos. R.O., D 137/767, 775).

Large numbers of out-and-out rogues, including pickpockets, footpads, swindlers, cheats, and those imposters whom Henry Mayhew in his exhaustive survey of rogues in *London Labour and the London Poor* was later to categorize as 'disaster beggars', led a wandering life. Some of them appeared regularly in Gloucester at fair-time, when the *Journal* issued its warnings in an attempt to cut their profits (no. 164–5, 170). A nice example of a much higher class of rogue is provided by the account of the female confidence trickster, travelling in style and naturally choosing one of Gloucester's two leading inns, the Bell, as her target (no. 167).

The number of people who took to a life on the roads to escape from personal problems in their settled existence or simply from the claustro-phobic pressures of village or small-town life is indicated by certain types of items that make regular appearances in the *Journal*. These are the notices inserted by parish officers advertising after absconded fathers of families, husbands after errant wives, masters after servants, tradesmen after apprentices, and recruiting-officers after those who took the king's shilling as a way out only to regret their decision and desert (nos. 159, 162). Under the rigid poor-law system those who absconded from their place of legal settlement would have little chance of gaining a new settlement in any other parish, and would in many cases be absorbed into the wandering population. The notices by the parish officers included here are interesting for the indication of the new roles adopted by the absconders – as ballad-monger, hedge-preacher, navvy on the turnpike roads, and casual harvest-worker (nos. 158, 160, 163). No. 173 illustrates the heartless way the system was enforced by some overseers of the poor, obsessed with moving vagrants on, over the parish boundary.

155 *30 August 1737*

> Yesterday the . . . following Malefactors were executed here (*i.e.* Gloucester), viz. Abraham Wood and John Wood, two Gypsies, for robbing Henry Lovel, on the Seven Downs of this County, of 40s. in Silver, and 16d. in Brass. They both deny'd the Fact . . .
>
> N.B. The Paper left by Abraham Wood will be inserted in our next, that the World may be acquainted with the Lives and Actions of those infamous Strollers call'd Gypsies

6 September 1737

Pursuant to our Promise, the following is a Copy of the Paper left by Abraham Wood, a Gypsy, who was executed here on Friday the 26th past, for robbing Henry Lovel (another Gypsy) on the Highway.

The Way of Life those Strollers, who call themselves, Egyptians, lead. In one Gang belonging to the Lovells and Bozells, there are thirty; and when they meet together, some strike out one way and some another, to 'spy out Gentlemens and Farmers Flocks of Sheep, and in the Night-time meet together again, and steal the best they can find, and what Quantity they please, by catching 'em with a Dog; and when they come to a Place convenient, they skin them and draw them, and bury the Skins and Guts, or throw 'em into a Pool of Water and sink them with Stones. They carry the Carcases 6 or 7 Miles in the Night-time from the Place they steal them; then they get into some secret Place, and tear Hedges, or get any thing they can first lay their Hands on, and make a Fire, and Roast and Boil till

Received   Bro'over   1334 | 10 | 3

1777
Dec'r 19   Of Farmer James for a Year's Rent of a Ground due Mich'.t last ——   2 | 0 | 0

1778
Apr. 16   Of Farmer Smith half year's Rent due Michaelmass last ——   60 | 0 | 0

Oct 16   For the Use of the lower part of the Ten Acres for Welch beasts 1 Night   2 | 11 | 6

Nov: 13   Of Farmer Shurmur half year's Rent of Tythes due Lady day last   60 | 0 | 0

Apr. 3 1779   Of Farmer James for a year's Rent of a Ground due Mich't last ——   2 | 0 | 0

15.   Of Farmer Smith half years Rent due Mich't last ——   60 | 0 | 0

Aug: 24   For the Use of the upper part of the ten Acres for one night for 100 head of Cattle   01 | 10 | 0

Oct 23   For the Use of the Ten Acres (the lower Part quite fresh) for Welch Cattle one night   2 | 10 | 0

Nov: 6.   Received of Farmer Smith half a Year's Rent of the Tythes of Barnsley due old Lady day last, according to the new agreement of 190£ per Ann. to commence from old Mich't 1778 ——   95 | 0 | 0

£   1620 | 1 | 9

Accounts of the Revd. Charles Coxwell, rector of Barnsley, 1777–9, including payments for pasture by cattle drovers using the 'Welsh Way'.

they have devour'd what they have; often in the mean time some strike out and steal a Horse or two, and some upon the Highway. About six Years ago, this Lovell and some of his Gang stole three Horses near Tamworth; one of them was a bright bay cropt Gelding; and a Hue-and-Cry was out after them, and they escap'd by getting into a Wood and going off by Night: The Men's Names that stole the Horses, are Henry Lovell the younger, and Thomas Lovell his Brother, and one Barnaby and Jeffery, Confederates together with Lovell's Gang. The names of the Bozells that belong to the same Gang, are John Bozell the elder, and his four Sons, viz. Peter, John, George, and William. The said John Bozell's Way of Life is mostly in pretending to tell Fortunes, and fraudulently getting People's Money by telling them, that by giving him such a Sum of Money, in such a Place they shall find a great Sum, and has brought a great many ignorant People to Ruin. There is one Geo. Kemp, who very often robs on the Highway; he is a tall well-looking Man, and pretends to have a Licence, and sells flower'd Waistcoats: Last Summer he broke open a House at Cely in Glamorganshire, and stole from thence six Gold Rings, and got off for Bristol: He most commonly has four Women dress'd very well along with him. Confess'd Aug. 21, 1737, by me,

Abraham Wood

156 *18 September 1753*

(in an advertisement for the owner of a stolen horse) . . . a Person, who calls himself George Steel, a thin pale Man, much pitted with the Small-pox, about 28 Years of Age, and about five Feet eight Inches high, and who says he was born at Chapel on the Hearth (*sic*), near Chipping-Norton, in Oxfordshire, of Travelling Parents, and that he has lived Four Years a Servant at Maidstone, in Kent, was, on the 4th Day of this instant, committed to the Castle at Gloucester, by Tho. Liston, Esq; on Suspicion of stealing a Dark-brown Gelding . . .

157 *6 August 1754*

Whereas Mary, the Widow of Thomas Collins, late of the Parish of Mitchel-Deane, in the County of Glocester, Mill-wright, goes begging about the Country, under Pretence of procuring Money to get her (late) Husband out of St. Briavel's Prison; This is to acquaint the Public, That her Husband has been dead these Two Years, and that her Family is man-tained by the aforesaid Parish.

N.B. She is a bold, Abusive Woman, and has lost her Fore Teeth; and she carries with her a counterfeit Pass signed by several Persons of bad Characters.

158 *26 November 1754*

Whereas William Belcher, Broad-weaver, (but of late Years a Methodist teacher) and William Shipway, jun. Wooll-Scribbler, both of the Parish of

Rodborough, in the County of Glocester, have some Time past, absented themselves, and left their respective Families chargeable to the Parish aforesaid; This, therefore, is to give Notice, That whoever will discover to the Officers of the said Parish where the said William Belcher and William Shipway are now residing, so that they, or either of them, may be apprehended and brought to Justice, shall receive from the Officers of the said Parish One Guinea for each of them, as soon as they, or either of them, shall be apprehended as aforesaid.

> WM. HALLIDAY, ⎫
> PETER MORRIS,   ⎬ Churchwardens
> DANIEL PEGLER, Overseer

Note. The said William Belcher is a short, pert-looking Man, about 50 Years of Age, and had on, when he went away, a Light-coloured Coat and a Brown Wig; and the said William Shipway is about Five Feet Nine Inches in height, near 40 Years of Age, has a thin Face, has formerly been in his Majesty's Service, and had on, when he went away, an old Red Coat (Part of his Regimentals) with a Badge of Grease round the Shoulders, and a short Brown Wig, and has lately been seen going about with Ballads.

28 March 1758

(*in a similar advertisement by the Rodborough overseer offering a reward for William Belcher and another man*) . . . The said William Belcher is a pert-looking Man, between Fifty and Sixty Years of Age, about Five Feet high, and hath been seen in or near Bristol, going about preaching, and also near Marshfield, going about with a Woman who sells Pedlars' Ware, and who is remarkable for having a thick Skin growing up between her Fingers so that she cannot easily clinch her Hand. He has been gone about Four Years.

159 *6 September 1757*

Deserted, from a Recruiting Party belonging to the First Division of Marines, at Stroud, in the County of Glocester, the 17th past, RICHARD KINGSBURY, born in Somersetshire, aged 29 Years, Five Feet Five Inches high, of a Black Complexion, with Black Hair and Eyes.

Also Deserted from the above Party at the same Time, ROBERT MOURE, born in the Parish of Stroud, aged 45 Years, Five Feet Eight Inches high, of a Black Complexion, with Black Hair and Eyes.

Whoever will secure the above Deserters, or either of them, and give Notice thereof to Capt. Thomas Eycott, at Cirencester, shall, for each of them, receive Forty Shillings Reward.

160 *14 October 1760*

Whereas George Adey, of the Parish of Horsly, in the County of Glocester, Broad-Weaver, did, about Easter last, abscond from his Family, and left the same chargeable to the said Parish of Horsly: This is to give Notice, that any Person or Persons who will apprehend the said George Adey, and bring him to the Churchwardens or Overseers, or one of them, or give Notice by Letter or otherwise, so as he can be brought to Justice, shall receive One Guinea Reward of us,

ALEX. DAVIS and JOHN GILMAN, Churchwardens.
EDWARD SMITH and JOHN HARVEY, Overseers.

N.B. The said George Adey is about Five Feet Three Inches high, talks a little lisping, of a swarthy Complexion, pitted with the Small-Pox very much about the Nose, with a great Scar on his Upper Lip, and has Two very remarkable Broad Teeth Before some Distance apart more than common; and wore a Wig. He is supposed to be at Bath, or somewhere at Work on the Turnpike-Roads adjoining.

161 *25 January 1779*

CAINSCROSS, Glocestershire.

Whereas on Thursday Evening the 21st Instant, four Men, who go by the Names of James Simson, Francis Jones, Samuel Chedworth, and Thomas Johnson, came into my House, and beat me and my Sister, broke the Windows and Doors, and afterwards threatened to murder us: Whoever will apprehend either of the above Men, so that they may be brought to Justice, shall have a handsome Reward from me.

THOMAS COSHAM.

N.B. They left a Bull Dog with a Collar on, Inscription *Joseph Bullus, Stourbridge.*
These men worked at the Stroudwater Navigation.

162 *8 May 1780*

Deserted on the 4th Instant, from Serjeant Eborall, recruiting for the Jamaica Volunteers at Minchinhampton, in the County of Glocester, WILLIAM GEORGE, a Welshman, by Trade a Labourer; two or three Years ago he used to travel this Country with a Stallion; he is about 27 Years of Age, five Feet six Inches high, wears his own short dark-brown Hair cut in the Soldier's Uniform, with a swarthy Complexion, dark Eyes, a small Scar on his Forehead, and a remarkable Scar on his Breast; had on when he deserted a Serjeant of Marines Frock with no Lace, light-coloured ragged Waistcoat, new Leather Breeches, brown Stockings, and plated Buckles, and an old round Hat: Whoever apprehends the above Deserter, and lodges him in any of his Majesty's Gaols, shall receive Half a Guinea Reward, besides his Majesty's Bounty for apprehending Deserters, by applying to Serjeant Eborall, at the Ram Inn in Minchinhampton.

WILTSHIRE.

Ran Away, and left his wife and family chargeable to the parish of Kemble, in this county, JOHN LOCK, of Ewen, in the said parish, cordwainer, supposed to be making for some sea-port with intent to go to a foreign part, and it is presumed he intends working on his way there as a harvest man and occasionally at his trade . . .

164 *29 November 1784*

As many unwary people will probably attend the fair held in this city to-day, it may not be improper to set them upon their guard; as we have had certain information that several sharpers and pickpockets will be there about two in the afternoon. Farmers are admonished to have a proper caution against all offers of civility from strangers, who may pretend to be acquainted with the parson of their parish, or come from the same part of the country with themselves and want to send a letter. Let them beware also of trusting their horses, &c. into the hands of strangers, before they have received the money for them. Some people will be robbed in the evening, and we therefore recommend caution in taking large sums in their pockets. Our information says, the road to Tewkesbury and Cheltenham will be the most dangerous. The vigilance of our magistrates has deterred these miscreants from coming near the city, as they used to do, the evening before the fair; they therefore lay concealed in the little alehouses around the country, till they can approach unsuspected in the guise of country people. The Sandhurst farmers are advised to go home in a body. All who make too free with the glass, will certainly be watched and waylaid.

6 December 1784

The hint given in our last to set the country people on their guard at the fair held here on Monday, was attended with the best effect possible. The sharpers and pickpockets came about the middle of the day in great numbers; but they found every one on the watch. The pockets were all buttoned close. No cullies to be met with. Several attempts were made to play the old game; but the gudgeons would not bite. The mayor's officers were very alert; and when any suspicious person appeared in the public-houses, a whisper went round to mark him. The keepers of turnpikes say they never saw so many farmers return perfectly sober from a fair. They all set off in parties before night, and being well armed with sticks, were prepared for each others defence. Three footpads, we are assured, were on the Tewkesbury, and two upon the Cheltenham road; but they had not resolution to make one attack.

165 *3 October 1785*

The number of cheats, who formerly attended our fairs, have been greatly diminished by the vigilance of our magistrates. When the practice of searching previous to a fair all the mean lodging-houses was first begun, a group of 40 or 50 of these vagrants were generally apprehended; but in the search made last week on the night before Barton Fair, not a person of this stamp was to be met with in or near the city . . .

166 *20 November 1786*

The public are cautioned against the imposition of a man, who rambles the country, pretending that he has sustained great loss by a fire at Cam, in the month of October last. The name of this imposter is Tho. Duddle. The person on whom the weight of this calamity fell, was Philadelphia Hill, a widow of Cam.

167 *2 March 1789*

A female adventurer, about three weeks ago, passed though this city, on a tour to raise contributions on the innkeepers, whom she pillaged to a considerable amount. On her arrival here, she drove into the Bell Inn in an elegant carriage, attended by her maid and a smart footman on horseback. The servant stiled her *Lady Hall.*

When Mr. Philpotts shewed her into the parlour she enquired for Mr. Pitt the Member; asked if he was in Glocester; adding that he was her near relation; and being told he was gone to take his seat in Parliament, she said she must write a card of congratulation to his Lady. The card was written in the presence of Mr. Philpotts, and her own servant dispatched with it. The waiter offered to shew the man the house, but he told him he had a tongue in his head, and should be at no loss to find it. Whilst her servant pretended to go on this errand, she produced a bill for fifteen guineas, for which she desired cash, which was given without hesitation. The servant quickly returned with a card, which he pretended to have brought in answer to her Ladyship's; and after taking a little refreshment, horses being ordered to her carriage, this fictitious lady of fashion drove off for Northleach. In the course of a week the bill for which Mr. Philpotts had given cash was returned as a forgery. It is described to us as a copper-plate, with the word *"Winchester"* at the top.

Since the discovery that the bill was a forgery, it appears that this female sharper was provided with several copper-plate notes; one was stiled the *Stratford Bank.* At Marlborough she put off a bill for 30 guineas; at Rodborough one for 20; at Northleach one for 30; at Burford one for 30.

The people who saw her represent her as a very beautiful woman, about 24 years of age, tall and genteel in person, and in manners very engaging.

A gentleman who lately came from London says, it is discovered that this scheme was projected by two noted Swindlers, one of whom acted the

Market traffic passing St. Nicholas church in Westgate Street, Gloucester, 1827.

part of the lady's maid; and the other the footman. The latter was a tall well-looking man, six feet high.

168 *4 May 1789*

NEWNHAM, Glocestershire,
April 28, 1789.

Apprehended here this day, John Brown and James Moore, wandering and begging about, who, upon their examination, not being able to give a good account of themselves, were committed as rogues and vagabonds to the house of correction at Glocester.

JOHN BROWN appears to be a sailor, about 24 years of age, five feet eight inches, says he came from Folkestone, in Kent, smooth-faced, short black hair, wears a blue jacket and petticoat trowsers, and a round hat, with small round brass shoe buckles.

JAMES MOORE says he is by trade a taylor and staymaker, served as a labouring bricklayer for several years past, appears to be about 37 years of age, five feet three inches high, thin pale visage, long dark brown hair, knock knee'd, wears a light coloured cloth coat, dark coloured waistcoat, with old leather breeches, and says he came from Litchfield, in Staffordshire.

As it appears from the conduct and examination of these men, that they have been for a considerable time past travelling about the country, without the least appearance of getting their livelihood by honest means, there may be some persons who may have reason to complain of their conduct in a criminal manner, it is therefore thought necessary to inform the public, that they may be seen upon an application at the County Gaol at Glocester.

169 *7 February 1791*

A SWINDLER.

Whereas Leonard Darke (a Strolling Rat Catcher) stands charged, and is committed to Aylesbury Jail, for defrauding a tradesman of Goods in Buckinghamshire, under false pretences, in the name of the Earl of Berkeley, and as it is imagined he has done the same in the county of Glocester, and parts adjacent, this is to request all persons so defrauded, to send an account of the transaction, in a letter, addressed to the aforesaid Earl of Berkeley, in Grafton-street, London.

170 *3 October 1796*

To the credit of the police of this city, four imposters, pretending themselves lame, were taken up during Barton Fair, and on Friday were severely flogged at the cart's tail. By this wholesome discipline our city is kept more free from vagrants than most other places in the kingdom.

113

171 *10 October 1796*

Whereas I, Thomas Jones, of Oxhall, in the county of Radnor, Gent. did violently assault and beat, aided by eight others, my drovers, without provocation, at one o'clock of the morning of the 22d August last, John Walker, Esq; Lord of the Manor of Guiting Power, otherwise Lower Guiting, in the county of Glocester; of which offence I was convicted before Powell Snell, Esq; and bound down to the next General Quarter Sessions; I do now hereby acknowledge the greatness of the offence, and for myself and my servants beg pardon of the said John Walker, Esq; and thank him for stopping this prosecution, on condition that I reimburse him his expences, and also deposit Ten Guineas for the use of the Poor of Lower Guiting aforesaid, not receiving Alms, at the discretion of the above Magistrate.

As witness my hand,

Stow-on-the Wold, Sept. 29   THOMAS JONES

172 *6 August 1810*

(*in a report of a series of fires at Summerwell Farm, near Tetbury, the property of a Mr. Rogers*)
. . . From the different places in which the flames burst forth, there can be no doubt of their being intentionally set on fire; and Mr. R. having a few days before impounded some horses, the property of a gang of gypsies in the neighbourhood, it is strongly suspected that these lawless banditti adopted this method of revenge.

173 *5 May 1817*

After the recent fatal consequences attendant upon the illegal removal of a pauper, named Godsall, from Twigworth to Tewkesbury, (and for which offence a bill of indictment was found by the Grand Jury at our last Assizes), we had hoped that we should not soon have had to notice another instance of a similar nature; but the following acccount has been handed to us: On the morning of Saturday s'ennight, a poor weather-beaten mariner was discovered lying in a ditch into which he had fallen, in the parish of Sandhurst, in the vicinity of this City, and was extricated from his perilous situation, in almost a lifeless state, by a gentleman who accidentally saw him, and by whom he was placed under the care of some persons who undertook to send for the overseer of the poor. Towards the close of the day, however, the poor fellow had crawled so far as the Leigh, about midway between this city and Tewkesbury, the overseers of which place put him into a stable, where they suffered him to remain all night with only a little hay to lie on, and a single blanket to cover him. On the Sunday morning he was informed that he must proceed on his journey, notwithstanding he earnestly entreated to be suffered to remain there and die. After proceeding a little way, he was unable to walk further, when the

114

overseers procured a horse, and conveyed him to Tewkesbury, where he arrived in a most debilitated state. The overseers of that borough, though he was brought in so illegal a manner, and during the time of Divine Service on Sunday, perceiving his helpless and miserable condition, ordered him to be immediately conveyed to the House of Industry, where proper medical aid, and every comfort which that well-regulated establishment afforded, was administered with promptitude; and where he now lies with very little hopes of recovery. The unfortunate man's name is Ellis Francis, a native of Clynnog, near Caernarvon, where his mother now resides on a small farm, and for which place he was now proceeding, after many years absence at sea. He was wrecked off the island of Madeira, on the 26th February last, in the Rebecca, Capt. Pricknipple, on his voyage from Jamaica to Liverpool, when the whole of the crew were drowned, except himself, the captain, and mate, who remained together on a raft eight and forty hours, and were then picked up by a Falmouth packet, and conveyed to port, where his two fellow-sufferers soon after died.

Showmen and Entertainers

This group of travellers needs little introduction, the various advertisers being only too able on their own account to describe with their customary hyperbole the 'curiosities', freaks of nature, or unusual performances they have to offer. The authentic voice of the showman delivering his spiel can be clearly heard in the extracts, and it will be seen that one of the necessary ingredients of such recitals was the claim of some connexion with royalty (preferably foreign) for the exhibit in question. In one case (no. 179) the exhibitor was trading on the current popularity of one particular foreign monarch, Frederick the Great of Prussia, England's ally in the war that was just then nearing its end.

Those featured here are only a small sample of the numerous types of travelling showmen and entertainers who used the *Journal* to advertise their impending arrival at some local inn, street-fair, or race-meeting. Many of the types are immediately recognizable from the literature of a rather later period – Henry Mayhew, and Dickens with his Crummles theatre company in *Nicholas Nickleby* and his wax-work proprietor and other show-people who figure in the *Old Curiosity Shop*. The notice of the inquest on the itinerant musician (no. 184) provides a poignant postscript to this group of travellers, many of whom must have died while still on the road, as poor as when they first started out.

174   *24 September 1734*

(*announcing entertainments during Gloucester races*) . . . And further, to divert the Gentry, Mr. Hurrell's Company of Comedians is come to Town, and intend to open next Tuesday Evening, at the Boothall, with the last new Comedy, call'd, *The Miser*, taken from Plautus and Moliere.

175   *7 February 1749*

They write from Cirencester, that, on Tuesday the 7th Instant, will be perform'd at the Play-House in that Town, for the Benefit of Mr. BOWMAN and Miss BROWN, (by a Company of Comedians from both Theatres in London) A CONCERT of Vocal and Instrumental MUSIC, divided into two Parts. Between which will be given gratis, A PLAY, call'd KING HENRY the Fourth, with the Humours of Sir John Falstaff: The Part of Falstaff to be perform'd by Mr. Linnett; King Henry, Mr. Hornby; Prince of Wales, Mr. Brown; Hotspur, Mr. Bowman; Worcester, Mr. Harman; Sir Walter Blunt, Mr. Fawkes; Sir Richard Vernon, Mrs. Brown (sic); Lady Percy, Mrs. Fawkes; and the Part of Mr. Quickby (sic), by Mrs. Linnett: with SINGING by Mr. Brown, viz. *On every Hill and every Grove*, &c. To which will be added an Entertainment call'd, The LOVERS' QUARREL. Being the last Night of Playing in that Town.

176   *6 November 1753*

Mr. Motet begs Leave to acquaint the Public, That the great Encoragement he has met with from the Curious of Cirencester and that Neighborhood has determined him to continue at the Bull-inn, in that Town, 'till Saturday next, but positively no longer, to exhibit his Six Inimitable Pieces of MARBLE-SCULPTURE, which represent the Transactions of Our Saviour's *Life, from his Last Supper to his Resurrection*, in upwards of 400 Fine Figures in Relievo, were 27 Years in finishing, and designed as a Present for the French King, to adorn his Royal Chapel at Versailles, but were taken during the last War. On Monday the 12th Instant they will be removed to Mr. Tuck's, the Prince and Princess in Tetbury, afterwards to Mr. Pincott's, the Bell in Dursley, and then to Wotton Underedge, Bristol, &c.

177   *12 July 1757*

We hear from Burford, that there are arrived in that Town, the amazing DROMEDARY from *Persia*, and the lofty CAMEL, from *Grand Cairo*, which were landed at Dover the 4th of April last, and have since been shewn in London, to the Royal Family, and to most of the Nobility; and they are allowed, by Gentlemen belonging to the University, to be the greatest Rarities in this Nation. The Dromedary is the first that has been in the Kingdom for 52 Years past. This wonderful Beast has on its Back Two large Humps of firm Gristle, with Tufts of Hair round them, and can travel Six Miles an Hour with Nine Hundred Weight. The Camel is a young and lofty creature, Four Years old, near 22 Hands high, can carry considerably more than the Dromedary, has a peculiar Joint behind more than any other Beast, (his Legs bending Four Times under him) and is so docile that he lies down at the Word of Command. These Creatures can travel 12 or 14 Days without drinking. On Monday next they will be exhibited at Cirencester, and, after a short Stay there, will be brought to Cheltenham, and from thence to this City.

178 *28 June 1757*

Mr. POWELL, the Celebrated *Fire-Eater* from London, (who has so much astonished the World with his Performances) being arrived in this City, will perform at the White-Hart on Wednesday next, and every succeeding Evening that Week . . .

179 *1 November 1762*

(Never shown in England before, being lately arrived from Berlin) To be Seen at the Swan in the Northgate-Street, Glocester, The following Pieces of curious WAX WORK, as large as Life: 1. An exact and very striking Likeness of his Majesty the present KING OF PRUSSIA in his State Uniform. 2. One of the King's Body of Field Hunters, in his proper Uniform, delivering, as a Courier, Dispatches to his Majesty. 3. A Captain of the Red Hussars, belonging to Gen. Seeden's Regiment, in his State Uniform, holding in his Hand the Head of a Russian Calmuck Tartarian Savage, which he killed in a Skirmish. 4. A black Hussar, belonging to the Death's Head Regiment of Prince Henry of Prussia. Every thing may be closely viewed, but nothing touched.

Likewise, some curious Prints of his Majesty the present King of Prussia, drawn from the Life to be sold at 1s. and 6d. each.

To be seen from Ten in the morning 'till Ten at Night, at 6d. each Person; Children and Servants 3d.; Ladies and Gentlemen to pay at their Discretion.

The Publick are desired to observe, that the Owner of the above Wax-Work is the Maker, and was a Prussian Black Hussar; and he, with a Red Hussar, of Gen. Seeden's Regiment, will give their Attendance at the Door in their proper Uniform, to introduce the Company.

N.B. They will wait on any Gentleman, &c. to take off a Face, which they will do as natural as Life.

Saturday next will be the last Day of shewing.

180 *28 May 1770*

They write from Oxford, by last post, that of all curiosities that ever were exhibited in that city, none has met with such general approbation and esteem as *Maria Theresa*, the amazing Corsican Fairy, who has had the honour of being shewn three times before their Majesties. This most astonishing part of the human species was born in the island of Corsica, on the mountain Stata Ota; in the year 1743. She is only 34 inches high, weighs but 26 pounds, and a child of two years of age has larger hands and feet . . . She will be shewn at Mr Nelson's at the New-Inn in this city on Tuesday next.

181 *4 May 1778*

GLOCESTER.
For One Night only.

SIGNOR ROSSIGNOEL, the famous Copier of the finest Notes of the Feathered Tribe, will perform in a CONCERT at the Bell Great Room in this City, on Monday the 4th of May Inst. After the Concert will be a BALL. Tickets 2s. 6d. each to be had at the Bell.

By particular Desire, he will also perform on Thursday next the 7th of May, at the George in Stroud. Tickets to be had at the George.

182 *31 January 1780*

The beautiful ZEBRA, which was intended as a present for the King of Spain, but taken by two English privateers and brought to Bristol, and sold to the celebrated Mr. Astley, Riding Master, of London, and which is now exhibiting with universal applause in Bath, will be in Glocester in a few days; and we hear that the proprietor intends to oblige the Ladies and Gentlemen at TETBURY, STROUD, and PAINSWICK, by stopping one day at each place. This most beautiful animal has the pre-eminence of all the brute creation. Dr. Gouldsmith says, a sight of the Zebra plainly shews the works of the Creator to be both wonderful and marvelous.

Notice of the arrival of this great curiosity will be given in our next.

183 *29 September 1794*

GLOCESTER.

The Stupendous PELICAN of the WILDERNESS, which has attracted so much the attention of the curious in the capital, is now to be seen at BARTON FAIR; also a very large COLLECTION OF WILD BEASTS; among which are, the Beautiful ASIATIC PANTHER, and the SEA LION, and a variety of other Rare Animals, never before seen in this city.

BY PERMISSION.

To be SEEN, during the FAIR, in a commodious CARAVAN, in Barton-street, an extraordinary Lusus NATURAE, just arrived from the GLASSIERES, in the grand Mountain of CHAMOUNI, the *two surprising Brothers*, called

THE ALBINOS:
who were honoured with a visit by their Majesties and the Royal Family at
Weymouth, on Wednesday August 20th 1794, and who were pleased to
express the highest satisfaction at the sight of those extraordinary persons.
Known and described by M. SAUSSURE in his journey to Chamouni, and
published in the *Encyclopaedia Brittanica*.

They have had the honour to be presented to Sir Joseph Banks, President
of the Royal Society in London.

They are allowed by gentlemen of the first science to be the most curious
phaenomena of nature's production. The hair of their heads is as white as
snow, and as strong as horse's hair; it flows over their shoulders, and has a
most beautiful appearance. Their eye-brows, eye-lashes, and beards are
also perfectly white: The skin of their heads is of a fine pink colour: Their
eyes are of a pale red, with a continual motion, like the pendulum, of a
clock. They can scarcely see by day, but have the advantage of seeing by
night: They are remarkably fair and ruddy, and of a pleasant countenance;
their manners sweet; and have a common education.

Dr. Munro, Professor of Anatomy, at Edinburgh, has minutely inspected
these men, and allows them to be real natural curiosities, and worthy the
attention of the curious.

184 *21 April 1806*

On Wednesday se'nnight an inquest was held by W. Trigg, Gent. at
Preston, near Cirencester, on view of the body of William Ryley, who was
found dead on the high road leading to Fairford. He had travelled the
country with musical bells for 45 years; and it is supposed, being 71, he
sunk under the pressure of poverty and infirmity. Verdict, *Died by the
Vistation of God.*

185 *28 September 1818*

NOW IN GLOUCESTER,
THE WONDER OF THE PRESENT AGE.
Under the Patronage of the Royal Family and the First Nobility.
TOBY, the SAPIENT PIG,
From the Royal Promenade Rooms, Spring Gardens, London.

This most surprising Creature will Spell and Read, Cast Accounts, tell the
Points of the Sun's Rising and Setting. Any Lady or Gentleman may put
Figures in a Box, and make what numbers they please, and then shut up
the box, and this wonderful Pig will absolutely tell what number is made
before the box is opened.

He will tell any person what o'clock it is, to a minute, by their watch; tell
the Age of any one in company; and, what is more astonishing, he will
discover a Person's Thoughts! And when asked a Question, will give an
immediate Answer.

In fact, he is beyond every conception, and must be seen to be believed. He is the only *Scholar* of his race ever known to be heard of in the world.

An elegant Place is prepared for the scene of his Exploits, adjoining the Turnpike Gate, Barton-Street, Gloucester.

Commences each day during the Fair, at the following hours, viz One, Two, Three, Four, Five, and Six.

Admittance, One Shilling.

CHAPTER SIX

The Dangers of Travel

Death, disaster, and discomfort inevitably figured largely in road travel as it was reported in the *Gloucester Journal* during the 18th century. The vast majority of journeys, passing without incident, ending on schedule at the proper destination, and for many travellers providing even some pleasurable experiences – as they bowled along on the top of a stagecoach on a fine spring morning or dined well in a wayside inn on a winter's day – must be left to the imagination. It was those journeys that ended in accident, robbery, or adverse weather conditions that made news for the *Journal*.

Robbery with Violence

That the exploits of highwaymen made popular reading was recognized by the editor of the *Journal*, who at times allowed his local news section to read like the *Newgate Calendar*. The long reports of such incidents, with their detailed descriptions of the villains, were of course intended partly to warn the public and to aid in the identification and capture of the offenders (as happened in the case in no. 186), but many of the incidents are related with an obvious relish and appreciation of their entertainment value.

Most of the provincial highwaymen who operated in Gloucestershire do not, however, accord with the popular notion of the stylish, gentlemanly villain, robbing the rich on the heaths around London. It is true that the Edgeworth highwayman of no. 187 approximated in dress, at least, to the popular idea, and that the man who cut his own throat at Bisley showed the appropriate desperate bravado, but the usual local type is probably best represented by the shabby couple, with no boots and riding stolen horses, who met Richard Selfe on the Tetbury road (no. 191). The bulk of the robberies reported were in any case the work of the more prosaic footpads, commonplace thugs who preyed mainly upon the poorer class of foot-traveller, often risking the gallows for very little reward.

The county had its popular 'robbing places', among them two lonely stretches of upland road mentioned in the following extracts, Ermin Street between Birdlip and Cirencester and the old Stroud-Cirencester turnpike east of Minchinhampton. The latter was the scene of several other incidents reported in the *Journal* at the same period (e.g. 9 May 1774; 30 Sept. 1782) and can claim a history of highway robberies dating back to 1371 when a gang of robbers lay in wait for merchants using that route (*Calendar of Patent Rolls*, 1370-4, 378). Many attacks, however, occurred at the approaches to towns, at places like Kingsholm and Saintbridge, near Gloucester.

186 *4 July 1763*

We have received the following particulars of a most audacious villain that has this week infested the roads between this place and Bath. On Wednesday morning he attacked, near the Monument on Lansdown, two persons, whom he robbed of some small sums; and afterwards coming to the turnpike on this side the down, he found there a man who was paying for passing through; on which the highwayman ordered the turnpikeman to go into his house and shut the door, or he would blow his brains out, saying "I'll receive the gentleman's money," and accordingly robbed the person of a considerable sum. He then came on to a little alehouse on the cross-road, where he put up his horse, and staid half an hour; and having drank a quart of strong beer, and fed his horse, he told the landlord he should set off for Tetbury. Upon the road, near Petty France, he robbed a gentleman's servant of eight guineas; and soon after meeting with a man returning from Tetbury market, near Dunkirk, he demanded his money. The man, who had a little boy before him, told the villain that he had none. He then demanded his watch, and endeavoured to pull it out of his pocket by the string, which in the struggle broke; and the man refusing to give it him, he said, "Do you contest with me?" and immediately putting his pistol over the boy's shoulder fired it, and lodged three slugs in the poor man's breast, of which he died soon after. The villain was immediately pursued by some people who heard the report of the pistol, but got clear off.

The landlord of the house where he baited says, he is a short young man, about 18, pitted much with the small-pox, well mounted on a dark-brown mare, which is blind of one eye, and has a switch tail. One of his stirrups is new, the other an old one.

25 July 1763

On Saturday about noon a man came to a blacksmith's shop in Chalford-bottom to have his horse shod; some people who happened to be present thought that he exactly answered the description which we gave in the paper of the highwayman who shot the man upon the Bath road about three weeks ago; they then surveyed his mare, and perceived that also to correspond with our account of it; upon which they immediately seized him, and in his pockets found a brace of pistols loaded with gravel-stones and bits of lead, which confirming their suspicions they carried him directly before a justice, who committed him to the care of the constable, by whom he was secured at the George in Bisley. The noise of a highwayman being taken brought many people to see him, and amongst the rest a man who had been robbed near Cirencester that morning. This person coming into the room when the highwayman was at supper, immediately declared, that he was the fellow who robbed him in the morning. *And will you swear that*, said the highwayman? To which the other replied strongly in the affirmative. *Why then*, says the villain, *I may as well die first as last*; and with the knife, with which he was eating his supper, cut his throat in a shocking manner. He was not dead yesterday morning, but it was thought he could not live 'till night. He has committed many robberies between Cirencester, Malmesbury, and Tetbury; and had in his pocket, when taken, about eight guineas. It is very fortunate this desperado is apprehended, as it is imagined he was crossing over to intercept the traders on their road to Bristol fair.

187 *18 April 1774*

Wednesday last Mr. Richard Neest, of Stroud, was robbed of a guinea and a shilling, in the parish of Edgeworth, in this county, by a highwayman well mounted on a bright-bay mare, with a few white hairs on her near foot before. The robber looked to be between 30 and 40, was marked with the small-pox, and had a scar upon his chin; and wore a light fustian frock, green waistcoat and breeches, a light two-curled wig, and a fan-tailed hat.

188 *8 September 1777*

A HIGHWAY ROBBERY

About Half an Hour after Seven, on Wednesday Evening, the 3d of September Inst. two lusty Footpads, armed with Horse-Pistols, attacked Mr. William Capel, in a Chaise, about the Seven-Mile Stone from Cirencester to Minchin-Hampton, and robbed him of about eight Guineas in Money, and a Silver Watch, Maker's Name *W. Dicks, Warminster*, No. 112; also of a handsome Steel-mounted Gun, with a Gold Touch-Hole, and a new bolted Lock, Maker's Name *Godsall*. And what is remarkable, the Metal of the large Part of the Barrel, for about five or six Inches, is of a different Colour from the other Part.

One of the Fellows had on a light coloured Frock, believed to be Russia Drab, very dirty; the Dress of the other not so well known, but thought to be of a dark Colour: Whoever will apprehend the said Footpads, or either of them, so that he or they may be brought to Justice, shall, on Conviction, receive TWENTY GUINEAS Reward, over and above that allowed by Act of Parliament.

WILLIAM CAPEL

Traffic on Westgate bridge, Gloucester, 1792.

30 March 1778

On Friday last Thomas Smart and Samuel Warren, for robbing Mr. Capell (*sic*) on the highway, were executed here pursuant to their sentence.

189 *8 December 1777*

The roads around this city are much infested with robbers, who attack passengers about the close of the evening . . .

190 *15 December 1777*

On Thursday evening last as the servant of —— Morgan, Esq; of Hempstead, near this city, was coming to town, he was stopt near Mrs. Lysons's gate by two footpads, who obliged him to dismount, he told them he had only three-pence in his pocket, which upon searching him they found to be true, and then giving him a penny to pay the pike, they took two-pence and dismissed him . . .

191 *21 September 1778*

On Tuesday evening last Richard Selfe, Esq; and his lady, returning from a visit, in an open carriage, were robbed about two miles from Cirencester, in the Tetbury road, by two highwaymen, with handkerchiefs over their faces. The one was a tall lusty young man, in a blue surtout coat; the other rather short, and wore a duffil coat, with a crimson collar. Mr Selfe lost about three guineas: they refused his watch. The fellows had no boots on, and rode two horses which they had stolen in the neighbourhood: the one a black horse, from farmer Lyne, of Pool Farm; the other was a little brown horse, that belonged to a butcher at Hampton.

192 *8 October 1781*

The evening of Barton fair, two villains, who had observed in the public-houses in this city the farmers to whom sums of money had been paid, repaired to Wooldridge, and there waylaid and robbed them of considerable sums; from one they took 40l. from another 18 guineas, and they had even the meanness to take 1s. and 1s. 6d. from two poor labourers.

193 *24 March 1783*

Last Monday evening about seven o'clock two highwaymen robbed six or seven people between Cirencester and Birdlip. From Mr. Hayward of Brimpsfield they took ten guineas and a watch; from Mr. Bishop, of Birdlip, three guineas, and a watch; and upon his desiring a crown piece, for which he had a particular value, they returned it. Mr. Haviland, of Winstone; Mr. Goodwin, of Birdlip; and Mr. Pitt, of Witcomb, were all robbed. The last was very ill treated by the villains, who gave him a violent blow upon the head. They dismounted from their horses to search the pockets. They were traced through Cranham wood very near to this city.

194 *26 January 1784*

About three o'clock in the afternoon of Saturday the 17th instant, Ann Bishop, on her return from Stroud to Bisley, was robbed of three guineas in gold, and 48s. in silver, by a young fellow, that appeared about 25 years of age, rather short, light brown hair, and grey eyes, had on a blue coat and waistcoat, with a white pair of long trowsers. The fellow knocked her down, and stabbed her in the hand, on her endeavouring to prevent his cutting off her pockets, which he at last effected.

195 *23 October 1786*

On Wednesday morning last Mary Bethell, of Painswick, coming to this city, was attacked a little beyond St. Bridge, by two ruffians, who treated her with great cruelty, tearing her handkerchief from her neck, cutting off her pockets, and threatening to cut her throat. She describes the men as of short stature, very ill-looking fellows, and meanly dressed. They robbed her of ten half-crowns, two pocket-handkerchiefs, a pair of pockets, a white apron, and a pair of buckles. The poor girl was coming to Glocester to buy her a gown.

196 *18 January 1802*

On Saturday se'nnight, about eleven o'clock at night, as Mr. Legeyet, farmer, of Walsworth, was returning home from our market, he was met near Kingsholm turnpike by a footpad, who demanded his money; but Mr. Legeyet resisted his attacks, and would no doubt have been able to secure the villain, had not a second come up, who knocked the farmer down, and, assisted by his companion, beat him very severely, and rifled his pockets of about 20 guineas. Wm. Meads, a grenadier in the Oxfordshire Militia, quartered here, having passed a five-guinea bill in payment at the George Coffee-House, which Mr. Legeyet can swear to, Meads was in consequence taken up, and was on Tuesday last committed to our county gaol, on suspicion of being one of the robbers: the other is yet at large.

197 *10 October 1814*

Cock-Road Gang of Marauders. Information having been given to the Magistrates, that a gang of desperadoes infested the above neighbourhood, to such an alarming degree that no inhabitant was safe in his bed, and no traveller could, without danger, pass the Kingswood road, on Sunday evening last, a strong party of police officers from Bristol, were dispatched in order to take them into custody. The gang had, however, been apprized of their approach, and a desperate conflict ensued; some of the officers were severely wounded, and were obliged to retreat for that night. Early on Monday morning a much stronger force, well-armed, repaired thither, and succeeded in securing seven men and two women, who were immediately committed to Lawford's-gate Bridewell. Caines, (the principal ring-leader,) escaped, but his mother and his son were taken. Bales of stolen property were found concealed in their respective dwellings.

Road Accidents

The number of serious road accidents, not uncommonly involving loss of life, that the *Journal* reports, may surprise some modern readers who may imagine them to be a phenomenon of the motor age. Passengers in coaches which lost wheels or overturned at speed were lucky if they escaped without major injury, while another variety of accident that seems to have occurred fairly frequently involved coachmen and waggoners, overcome by sleep or drink, falling beneath their own wheels. Some of the most famous coach accidents were the result of coachmen from rival concerns racing or obstructing one another, either as a matter of personal honour or for the reputation of their employers (nos. 198, 207). The narrowness of many roads, even some of the main turnpikes, made minor accidents between vehicles trying to pass each other a regular occurrence. When a member of the gentry or one of the wealthier classes was the injured party legal action might be threatened, leading to the servile public apologies, of which nos. 199–200 are examples. Such an incident between two members of the poorer classes was no doubt often settled at the roadside by blows. In 1753 (6 Nov.) the *Journal* reported a battle for right-of-way that took place between some waggoners and some soldiers whose vehicles met on a narrow piece of road near Bromsgrove.

One group of road-users whose ill-fortune or fecklessness often gained them a place in the news reports were the farmers, whose traditional habit of heavy drinking on market days was the cause of many accidents. An extract quoted in another chapter (Chapter V, no. 164) records the surprise of the local turnpike-keepers at the sight of so many farmers returning sober from one of the Gloucester fairs, the result of a warning about footpads. The Hartpury farmer (no. 201) might have been forgiven for thinking that, however drunk, he could make it home safely along Over Causeway, but William Jones (no. 203), whose road home to his farmhouse on the Lancaut peninsula beside the Wye took him close to the edge of some of the steepest river-cliffs in the British Isles, had every reason to remain sober.

The New Inn, Gloucester, c. 1830. At this date the great 15th-century inn was no longer one of Gloucester's leading inns; its yard was used only by the carts of local carriers and market-traders.

198 *11 July 1774*

Whereas, it is industriously reported that Mr. Pruen's New Glocester Machine was overturned on Friday Night the 1st Inst. in its Way to London, by my Coachman wilfully and maliciously driving against it: I find myself under the Necessity of publishing the underwritten Affidavit, and do at the same Time intreat the Public, to judge of my Conduct for the future by their own Senses, and not by any Misrepresentations which may be speciously offered in order to interrupt and to avert that Encouragement which I have hitherto received, and which I desire to retain upon no other Conditions, than those of a fair, honest, and grateful Conduct.

JOHN TURNER

John Haines, of the City of Glocester, Coachman, Servant to Mr. John Turner, of the said City, Coachmaster, maketh Oath and saith, That on Friday Night the 1st of July Instant, he drove his said Master's Stage Coach from Glocester to Oxford, and that while he was watering his Horses at Crickley-Hill, Mr. Pruen's Coachman drove by him, and that he this Deponent soon after followed Mr. Pruen's Coach, without any Attempt or Intention to pass by it; that directly after passing through Cuberly Turnpike, Mr. Pruen's Coachman turned off to the Summer Road which lies at the left Hand of the Turnpike Road; and that he this Deponent kept on the said Turnpike Road, and that at the Time Mr. Pruen's Coach was overturned, he this Deponent was driving his said Master's Coach behind Mr. Pruen's Coach, at the usual Rate of travelling, and at the Distance of at least sixty Yards from it.

JOHN HAINES

Sworn before me this 9th of July, 1774, EDWARD BAYLIS

199 *18 January 1779*

Whereas I Richard Woolford, of Cirencester, in the County of Glocester, have been guilty of a most notorious Insult and Outrage in driving a Waggon against the Carriage of Thomas Master, Esq; of Cirencester, whereby very fatal Consequences had like to have ensued to some of that Gentleman's Family; for which he had most justly commenced an Action against me; but upon my earnest Solicitation for Pardon, and unfeigned Sorrow for my Offence, he has been pleased to stop the Prosecution, upon my making an Acknowledgment in the Glocester Journal, which I most thankfully comply with; as Witness my Hand

RICHARD WOOLFORD

200 *2 May 1785*

Whereas, as we James Wood and Thomas Jones, servants to John Scudamore, of the parish of Flaxley, were both riding in the waggon on the turnpike road near Glocester, we met the Rev. Mr. Roberts, of Monmouth, in his carriage, and refused to give proper room for him to go by, by that means the wheels of the waggon run against the horses; we also used Mr. Roberts with very abuseful language, so that he justly intended to bring us to justice, but has since shown compassion, and stopped all prosecution against us, we being very poor and have humbly asked his pardon in this public manner, promising never to be guilty of the like offence; as witness our hands this 18th of April, 1785.

JAMES WOOD
THOMAS JONES

201   *2 October 1786*

The number of country people, who have lost their lives within the last six months by going home from markets and fairs in a state of intoxication, has been very considerable in this county; yet the frequency of such accidents makes no impression. A farmer of Hartpury, returning on Thursday evening from Barton Fair, was so excessively drunk, that he fell from his horse over the parapet of Westgate Bridge into the Severn, and was drowned. The body could not be found till Friday night.

202   *15 December 1788*

Glocester Light Coach.

Whereas this Coach was overturned on the 26th of July last, about a mile from Henley upon Thames, in going from London to Glocester, by which accident one of the passengers had his leg broke, has been confined ever since, and is not now able to move without crutches. As there is great reason to believe, that the accident was owing to the carelessness of the Driver, the sentiments of the other passengers are desired before any steps are taken to punish the offender; This is, therefore, to request the said passengers will send a line addressed to the Printer of this paper, mentioning their place of abode, and they will be immediately waited upon. It is hoped this will be done without hesitation, as it is for the good of the public, that an example should be made of such offenders. The places taken in London were as follow:

> Mr. ANSELL,
> Mr. GODWIN,   } *Inside.*
> Mr. CROSDALE, two places,
> Mr. BAKER, *Outside.*

203   *25 April 1796*

On Friday last an inquest was taken on the body of William Jones, of Lancaut, in this county, Yeoman, by Mr. Joyner, of Berkeley. It appeared that Jones in a state of intoxication, returning home from Chepstow, on Sunday the 10th, missed his road in the night, and fell from the high Clifts that over-look the river Wye, opposite to Piercefield-house. The precipice in that place is not less than 50 yards high. The body was not discovered till last Wednesday evening, when some gentlemen and ladies of Chepstow, walking by the river side, discovered it mangled by vermin in a shocking state.

204   *10 November 1806*

On Thursday evening, about seven o'clock, as the Rev. Mr. Neale and family were returning home from the County Election, the carriage, although on the edge of the road, was furiously run against by an empty waggon, (the driver of which was intoxicated,) on the Cheltenham road, near the Hare and Hounds. By the shock, the hinder wheel, hinder spring, braces, and part of the axle-tree, were entirely carried away, and the carriage so much damaged, that it was with difficulty it could be got back to this city next morning. The family, however, sustained no personal injury; and Mr. and Mrs. Minster fortunately passing at the time, with great kindness took the ladies into their chaise. The same waggon was, a short time before, passed with difficulty and hazard, by some gentlemen near Staverton bridge; and as an action is commenced against the owner, the parties above alluded to would promote the public good, and their own future safety, by coming forward with their evidence on this occasion.

205   *22 December 1806*

Melancholy Accident. On Monday evening last, as the Bristol and Birmingham mail-coach was coming down the hill between Alveston and Thornbury, in this county, the coachman, John Fishlock, being much intoxicated, and the night very dark, fell from the box, and one of the wheels passing over his neck, he was killed on the spot. The guard, William Giller, observing the accident, instantly got down, and endeavoured to stop the horses; but, finding themselves at liberty, they got into full speed, and he was unable to effect his purpose. With great activity and presence of mind, however, he regained his place behind, whence he got to the box, and drove the coach in safety to Thornbury. Giller immediately returned on horseback, in search of the unfortunate man, who he found totally lifeless; and the Coroner's Inquest have since returned a verdict, *Accidental Death*. He has left a wife and two children.

206   *30 March 1807*

Whereas I, James Ravenhill, did on Monday, the 23d of February, kill a Pig by the side of the Bristol road, at which the horse of Thos. Smith, Esq. taking fright, his carriage was overturned and much injury happened thereto, and his own life exposed to imminent danger. And whereas the said Thomas Smith hath directed an action to be brought against me for the damages occasioned by my improper and unlawful conduct, unless I do publicly apologise for the same, and promise never again to be guilty of the like offence.

Stagecoaches of the early 19th century.

Now I do hereby beg Pardon of the said Thomas Smith, and of the Public, for my misconduct; and I do engage never again to offend in the same way.

JAMES RAVENHILL

207 *28 July 1817*

Dangerous Effects of Coach-Racing! On Thursday morning, about eight o'clock, the Gloucester and London Day-Coach, on its journey upwards, whilst racing with the Cheltenham Day-Coach, (both vehicles going at the rate of nearly twelve miles an hour,) was overturned within a short distance of Burford; when, as might naturally have been expected, not one of the passengers escaped unhurt! There were three outside-passengers; and, such was the force of the shock, that they were thrown several yards from the coach. Mr. Thos. Heath, of the City Arms, Oxford, who was on the roof, had his leg broken near the ancle, the joint of which, and the foot were so much torn and lacerated, that he was compelled to undergo amputation soon afterwards. The coachman (Bishop) was severely injured about the loins, and now lies seriously ill; and the other two were partially bruised. Of the inside passengers, (three ladies and a gentleman), one of the former was terribly cut in the face, having the under lip severed in two, and one tooth beaten out; and another the collar-bone dislocated, and sustained such serious contusions on other parts of the body, that she has been confined to bed ever since: the others also suffered severely. We have been the more minute in detailing these circumstances, because the injuries inflicted were solely and exclusively attributable to the misconduct of the coachman; and we cannot too forcibly reprobate the custom of racing so furiously on these occasions, by which the lives of the passengers who entrust themselves to their care are put in such imminent peril, merely to indulge the whim or the caprice of these infuriated drivers! In the present instance, we should ask, what adequate recompense can the proprietors of the coach extend to the unhappy sufferer who is thus rendered a cripple for life, through the wilful misconduct of their servant? In similar circumstances, it is not unfrequently attempted to justify the coachman by recurring to the instructions of his employers – 'to suffer nothing to pass him on the road, and not to spare horse-flesh!' In this case, however, we have too high an opinion of the proprietors to entertain so unworthy an idea of their conduct . . .

208 *17 July 1820*

Caution. Last week, Richard Jefferies, waggoner to Messrs. Tanner and Baylis, was committed to the House of Correction for three months, for intoxication, sleeping on the shafts of the waggon on the road, and neglecting to lock the wheels whilst going down a hill, in consequence of which the horses were thrown down, and three of them materially injured.

Bad Weather

The rather hackneyed Christmas-card scene of a stagecoach up to its axles in a snowdrift was fairly often a reality on the high Cotswolds, where even in our generally milder winters the motorist driving up from the Vale can suddenly find himself entering a different climate. More striking, however, are the sombre accounts of the fate of travellers on foot overtaken by appalling conditions on isolated stretches of road (nos. 211–12).

Away from the hills it was floods that more usually interrupted road traffic, as the Severn made one of its periodic attempts to regain its hold on a large part of the Vale. The most notable flood of the whole 100-year period was apparently that of November 1770 (no. 213) when small boats plied into College Green at Gloucester and many people were stranded in the upper rooms of their houses. Among the regular traffic of the roads that suffered on these occasions was the *Journal*'s own distribution network (nos. 209, 214). In 1782 the distributor of the paper in South Wales was drowned in a flood (*G.J.* 7 Jan. 1782).

209   *31 December 1734*

> The Waters being so very high, by reason of the great Quantity of Rain and Snow that has lately fallen, such of our Readers who may not receive the News so soon as ordinary, and others to whom, where the Roads are impassable, it cannot be brought this Week, will, we hope, be so candid as to excuse it.

210   *7 February 1749*

> They write from Burford that, on Saturday last, Sarah Savage, of Broad-Rissington, having, on her Return from Burford Market, lost her Way on the Downs, was found starv'd to Death near a Sheepfold.

211   *2 March 1762*

> We have received many melancholy Accounts of the unhappy Consequences of the violent Storm of Wind and Snow which happened Yesterday Se'nnight; but those from Stow on the Wold are the most affecting: A Party of about Eighty Recruits, belonging to the Regiment of Young Buffs, were on their March from Northleach; and when they had reached within the Distance of a Mile from Stow, the Severity of the Storm became so great, and the Intenseness of the Cold so sharp as to deprive them of the Use of their Limbs; and it was with the utmost Difficulty that the Officer, who was on Horseback, reached Stow; where he procured the Assistance of the Inhabitants, who sent Men and Horses to their Relief. Four of them

were found dead upon the Road, and another died soon after he was brought to Stow. They were all buried on Thursday in one Grave. The Benevolence and Humanity which the Inhabitants of Stow displayed upon this melancholy Occasion, deserve the highest Encomiums.

The same Day, the Post-Boy, near Fairford, fell with his Horse into a hollow Way which the Snow had filled up, and it was with the greatest Difficulty he disengaged himself from the Beast and walked to Fairford, where he was obliged to procure Assistance to dig his Horse out of the Snow. This was the Cause of the Post's being so late last Monday.

212 *22 January 1770*

We have accounts from several parts of the country, that the severe cold wind on Wednesday evening the 10th inst. had nearly killed many people who were exposed to it upon the road. The miller of Ablington, near Bibury, on his return home from Northleach market, lost his life. He was found dead the next day upon his knees, with his face to the ground as if blowing in his hands . . .

213 *26 November 1770*

The great flood upon this river is considerably abated, and though the meadows are yet under water the houses in this city and country, that were exposed to the inundation, are now free from it, and the people are returning to their dwellings. We have no tradition in this or the last century of the water having risen to such a height. It was eight feet deep upon the meadows, which is four feet higher than has ever been remembered. The water was so deep upon the high causeway between this city and Over that a barge sailed over it . . .

The Brecknock coach on Tuesday could come no nearer to this city than Highnam, from whence the passengers and goods were safely conveyed hither in a boat, and another coach immediately set off with them for London.

The Bristol road has also been so much under water that no carriages could pass. The stage coach has been stopped for this whole week.

As no horses could pass the water between this city and the other side of the river, the mails were brought over in boats, and the post-boys waited on the other side 'till the boats returned with the bags going downwards . . .

214 *14 March 1774*

Three such dismal days as Monday, Tuesday, and Wednesday last have scarcely been ever known in this climate. The rains on the two first days have occasioned an inundation that has only been exceeded by the great flood in 1770; the water rose so fast on Thursday, that it was feared we should have been as much overflowed as at that memorable time; but it

135

began to sink again on Friday, and in a few days we hope it will return to its usual channel. Nor were the hills less incommoded by Wednesday's snow than the vale by the floods, for the road between this and Cirencester was entirely blocked up for two days. The London post due on Thursday did not arrive 'till Friday evening, and four or five stage waggons, from London to this city, Hereford, and other places, were stuck fast at Nettleton Bottom between Birdlip and Cirencester for two days, the snow being as high as the tops of the waggons. The Bath road was also quite stopped. The Bristol postman was unfortunately drowned in the road near Hempstead, about two miles from hence; and a boy was found frozen to death on the Bath road near the Cross-hands. Edw. Vickers, who distributes this Paper through Worcester and Bromsgrove, in his return on Thursday, was by the violence of the wind blown horse and all from the high causeway, between Tewkesbury and the Mythe, into the flood; his horse swam with him for a quarter of an hour, and just as the poor beast was exhausted, a boat most providentially came and saved both the man and his horse. Our thanks are particularly due on this occasion to Wm. Buckle, Esq; of the Mythe, for his great humanity to the poor man.

A person from Guiting brings an account, that on Wednesday last Farmer Dowdeswell, of that place, having sent his son, with a servant man and boy, to take a load of barley to Winchcomb, the cold was so extremely severe on the hills, that Mr. Dowdeswell's son and two of the horses were frozen to death, and the man and boy are so benumbed, that their recovery is very doubtful.

215 *12 February 1816*

After some very variable weather, we had a heavy fall of snow on Tuesday afternoon and evening, whch lay to a considerable depth, and impeded travelling so much that the London mail of Wednesday did not reach this city till three hours after the usual time. At Enstone and Frogmill, the coach was compelled to leave the turnpike-road, and pass through the adjoining fields for a short way . . .

CHAPTER SEVEN

The Severn Passages

Although Gloucester was the only place in the county where the Severn was bridged, travellers could cross the river at nine or ten other places by means of the 'passages'. These were ferry services of varying degrees of safety and efficiency operated, by virtue of certain ancient rights, by the keepers of riverside inns which stood at the terminals of the passages. The four passages above Gloucester – at Ashleworth, the Haw, and the Upper and Lower Lodes at Tewkesbury – figure little in the pages of the *Gloucester Journal*, for they served only minor local routes of communication and, being on the safer, upper reaches of the river, were less prone to newsworthy accidents. The extracts printed here refer to the five regular crossing points below Gloucester – from Framilode to Rodley, from Arlingham to Newnham, from Purton in Berkeley parish to Purton in Lydney parish, from Aust to Beachley (the Old Passage), and from Redwick to St. Pierre in Monmouthshire (the New Passage). Another ancient passage, at Sheperdine in Rockhampton parish, had apparently gone out of use by this period (Rudder, *New History*, p. 628).

The most significant in terms of road transport were the two lowest passages, for they provided the chief links between Bristol and South Wales and in the late 18th and the early 19th centuries, when vehicles were carried on the boats, served coaching and mail routes. Both could, however be difficult and dangerous to negotiate, for the fierce tide of the Severn was funnelled between rocky shorelines and often aggravated in its effect by the prevailing south-westerly winds. Even the long detour by way of Gloucester was found preferable to crossing by some 18th-century travellers, among them Daniel Defoe who arrived at Aust in the course of his *Tour Through the Whole Island* (pp. 364–5) and wrote 'the sea was so broad, the fame of the Bore of the tide so formidable, the wind also made the water so rough, and which was worse, the boats to carry over both man and horse appeared . . . so very mean, that in short none of us cared to venture'. Thomas Telford, who made a survey of the mail-route into South Wales in 1823, described the New Passage as 'one of the most forbidding places at which an important ferry was ever established' (L.T.C. Rolt, *Thomas Telford*, 1958, Chapter 9).

Serious accidents to the boats at the Old and New Passages (nos. 217–20, 223, 226) were sufficiently frequent to have given the two crossings a dubious reputation by 1806 when the promoters of a new coach-service from London to Carmarthen by way of Gloucester headed their advertisement with the message: 'The Dangers and Disagreeables of The Passage over the Severn Sea avoided' (*G.J.* 20 Jan. 1806). The erratic timetable that wind and tide imposed on the passage-boats (no. 229) was an added deterrent, especially as, according to the *Gloucester New Guide* of 1802, missing one of the regular sailings could prove expensive: 'if there is a necessity of hiring a boat on purpose, the passenger will be at the mercy of a set of men who take every occasion of extortion, and what would have cost four-pence only, at the regular time, will be increased to half-a-crown at least, or perhaps, under various pretences, he may be detained at the inn till the next tide.' It was not until 1825, when a new company was formed to operate steamboats, that a determined attempt was made to improve the facilities at the Beachley passage (*V.C.H. Glos.* x. 54–5); wind and tide retained, however, their power to disrupt sailings and continued to do so even in the days of the diesel car-ferries which plied that route in the 20th century before the opening of the Severn Bridge.

The three passages further up river, at Purton, Newnham, and Framilode, were also used to some extent by long-distance traffic but mainly provided very local communication between the parishes on the Vale of Gloucester and Forest of Dean banks. Loss of life from accidents to the boats could occur at these passages too (nos. 228, 230) – all navigation on the tidal Severn was potentially hazardous – but more people it seems were drowned there while negotiating the sandbanks and shallows on foot or on horseback (nos. 222, 224). Both at Newnham and at Purton it was sometimes possible to wade the river at low tide, when it was in any case often necessary to take to the river bed in order to reach the passage-boats. The Revd. William Wickenden, who lived at Blakeney in the early years of the 19th century, has left a description of the complications of crossing at the Purton passage at low tide: it was necessary to wade a shallow channel near the passage-house on the Berkeley side and then walk for almost a mile down a ridge of sand in the middle of the river before coming opposite the passage-house on the Lydney side. Many people, says Wickenden, were drowned there through misjudging the time of the tide, and he gives a graphic account of a narrow escape that he himself had, when he had to race for his life back up the sandbank with the bore close on his heels (William Wickenden, *Poems and Tales*, 1851, pp. li–liv).

At Newnham the difficulties of the crossing encouraged an attempt,

138

begun in 1810, to replace it with a tunnel under the river. The promoters of the scheme had just successfully completed a pioneering railway tunnel on the nearby Bullo Pill tramroad, but their equipment and expertise proved inadequate for their ambitious new venture (nos. 231–2; *V.C.H. Glos.* x. 30).

Two of the extracts in this chapter (nos. 217, 224) illustrate the problems of accurate news-gathering in 18th-century England. Difficulties in checking the validity of the reports it received meant that the *Journal* had often to admit to printing what had turned out to be mere rumour or a garbled version of the facts. Sometimes, for example, a local person found himself prematurely obituarized and was obliged like Mark Twain to reassure acquaintances that 'the report of my death was an exaggeration.'

216 *6 March 1753*

We are assured that the Ferry, or Passage, called Pyrton-Passage, over the River Severn, is now as safe and commodious as it hath been known in the Memory of Man; and that Horse and Foot-passengers, and all Sorts of Cattle, may pass and repass at High and Low Water.

217 *12 October 1756*

From Bristol we have the melancholy News, that on Wednesday Night last the Old-Passage Boat, crossing the River Severn at Beechly, was overset in a Storm; by which Accident 22 Passengers, and 18 Horses, were drowned.

19 October 1756

As we were misinformed, last Week, in regard to the Number of Persons and Horses drowned in the Passage-Boat at Beechly, we think it necessary to give our Readers the following Particulars, which may be depended upon, viz. That there were on board Three Servants, and Six Horses, belonging to Mr. Talbot, of Margam; One Servant, and Four Horses, of Dr. Davenport's; Mr. Thomas Parry, Brother to Mr. Parry at the Rose-and-crown in Narrow Wine-street, and Mr. Powell, Clerk to Mr. Warren's Glass-house in Thomas-street, Bristol; besides Six Boatmen and Servants belonging to the Keeper of the Passage-house; and that it is not certain whether an old Man and Woman were on board or not: That out of the Twelve Horses Three swam to Shore, and were saved alive; and that Seven have been since taken up at Portshut. When the Boat left the Shore, the Wind blew at West; and before they were Half over, it blew hard at South.

218 *11 May 1767*

Samuel Hill, at the Old Passage at Beachley, Glocestershire, begs Leave to acquaint the Nobility, Gentry, Tradesmen, Graziers, and Others, That he

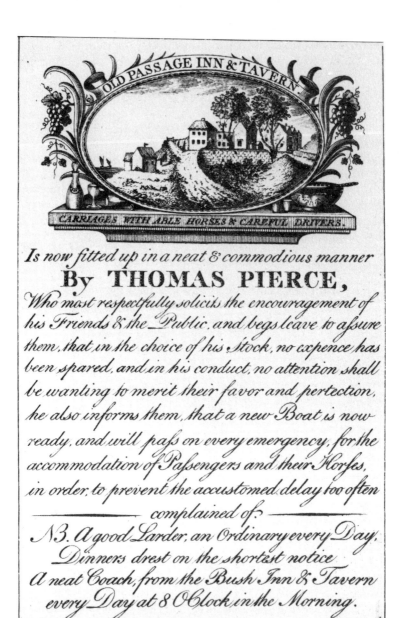

OLD PASSAGE INN & TAVERN

Is now fitted up in a neat & commodious manner

By THOMAS PIERCE,

Who most respectfully solicits the encouragement of his Friends & the Public, and begs leave to assure them, that in the choice of his Stock, no expence has been spared, and in his conduct, no attention shall be wanting to merit their favor and pertection, he also informs them, that a new Boat is now ready, and will pass on every emergency, for the accommodation of Passengers and their Horses, in order, to prevent the accustomed delay too often
——— *complained of.* ———
N.B. A good Larder, an Ordinary every Day, Dinners drest on the shortest notice A neat Coach, from the Bush Inn & Tavern every Day at 8 O'Clock in the Morning.

Innkeeper's advertisement for the Passage House at Aust.

has lately erected a Moveable Bridge six Feet wide, with strong Rails thereto, in order to be occasionally fixed alongside of the Passage Boats for the greater Safety and more expeditious Conveniency of loading all Manner of living Goods, &c. and with which Conveniency Horsemen may safely ride on board of the said Boats, without the least Risque or Danger: and furthermore desires to inform all Passengers in general, That, when any earnest Emergency requires, by making a Signal with Smoak, a small Boat shall instantly ply from the Beachley Shore to Aust Side for their speedy Conveyance over at any State of the Tide, when Wind and Weather will permit.

N.B. Neat Post-Chaises, and a genteel Post-Coach, with able Sets of Horses and careful Drivers, to any Part of England or Wales, upon the earliest Application to

Their most obedient and humble Servant
SAM. HILL.

219 *14 November 1774*

Whereas it has been industriously reported to my Prejudice, that the unhappy Accident on Sunday last, at the New Passage on the River Severn, happened at the Old Passage, and by Means of the Unskilfulness of my Boatmen: This is to inform the Public of the contrary, and that it always has and ever will be my Wish and Endeavour to furnish proper Boats, well found and manned, and in good Repair, and to exert my utmost Care for the Safety and Accomodation of all Passengers and their Effects.

Beachley, Nov. 10.   SAMUEL HILL.

220 *25 August 1777*

On Thursday last the passage boat was lost as she was crossing from Beachly to Aust; four boatmen and one other person, with 18 head of oxen and some horses, were drowned. The greater part of the passengers were luckily on board the small boat that was made fast to the stern of the passage boat, who, as soon as they saw the great boat likely to sink, had the presence of mind to cut the rope by which they were towed, and got safe to the shore.

221 *24 October 1785*

GLOCESTERSHIRE.
Newnham Passage Inn.

Daniel Edmonds (late of the Ship Tavern, Small-Street, Bristol) takes this opportunity of returning his warmest acknowledgments to his numerous friends for that countenance and support he has been honoured with, during a period of thirteen years; and respectfully informs them, and the public in general, that he has taken the above Inn at Newnham . . .

Dinners provided on the shortest notice. Wines and Spirits of the best quality. Post chaises with able horses. Passing boats kept in the best repair, with careful servants, &c.

222 *7 November 1785*

To the Public.

As a Paragraph lately appeared in the St. James's Chronicle, and other London Papers, that an Officer and his servant were lost in the sands near Newnham Ferry, I think it my duty to contradict the assertion in the most positive terms; and to inform the public, that such a paragraph was inserted merely with a view and design to injure the Passage and Ferry, and calculated on purpose to do me a real injury; it being a well known truth, that there never was an instance in the memory of the oldest man now living of any person losing his life at the Passage, or of any accident that ever happened there.

Newnham, Nov. 3.   DANIEL EDMONDS.

223 *11 September 1786*

A man who came to this city yesterday afternoon, relates, that in the stormy weather on Friday evening the small passage boat, in attempting to pass at Beachly, was by a squall of wind overset, and five passengers, with four boatmen, were lost.

224 *31 January 1791*

Monday last Mr. Price Richards, of Chepstow, endeavouring to cross a road, near Newnham, with his horse, the land-flood being very strong, he and his horse were carried down the stream, and drowned.

14 February 1791

It was Mr. Parry Richards, of Chepstow, (not Mr. Price Richards) who lost his life, (as lately mentioned in this paper) in attempting to ford the Severn at Purton. He was earnestly dissuaded, and told that the fresh in the river was too strong to be passed with any degree of safety; but he could not be prevailed upon to wait till the next morning.

225 *20 January 1794*

A Gentleman from Bristol relates a remarkable disaster that befel the Beachley passage boat about ten days ago. As the boat was coming over from the Monmouthshire side, a fog came on so thick, that the man knew not which way to steer, and they were carried up and down the river at the mercy of the tide, without being able to land their passengers for 36 hours; at last they reached the shore near Oldbury.

226 *25 December 1797*

Saturday morning last a melancholy accident happened on the river Severn. As one of the New Passage boats was returning from the Monmouthshire side, a sudden and most uncommonly violent squall of wind carried away her tackle, which rendered the vessel unmanageable, and caused her immediately to fill with water, whereby she sunk. There were six persons in her, five of whom perished, viz. three men and a boy belonging to the boat, and a genteel young man, a passenger, who had a small bundle with him. The master providentially escaped by getting into the small boat. The three boatmen that perished have left behind them three wives and near 20 children, who were solely supported by their industry.

227 *1 January 1798*

PYRTON PASSAGE, Jan. 1, 1798.

James Inman gratefully returns his Thanks for the many favours already conferred upon him, and begs leave to inform the Public, that the above Passage is rendered more commodious and certain, by well found Boats, able and careful Hands, and every attention paid to the speedy Conveyance of Passengers.
The Price for Passing as under:

			£. *s. d.*
			£. *s. d.*
Man and Horse,	.	.	0. 1. 0
A Horse,	.	.	0. 0. 9
Foot Person,	.	.	0. 0. 3
Horn Calves,	.	.	0. 0. 6 each.
Calves,	.	.	0. 0. 3 each.
Pigs and Sheep,	.	.	0. 2. 9 per score.

228 *6 February 1809*

On Thursday morning, between seven and eight o'clock, the passage boat which plies upon the Severn at Newnham, was swamped and sunk, when Mr. Hewlett, of Frampton, and the two boatmen, were drowned, in view of several spectators on both sides of the river, who, although they instantly put off in another boat, were not in time to render them any assistance. They had gone over to the opposite shore in the small boat, and were returning to Newnham to avoid the flood, when they were unexpectedly overtaken by the *bore*, or head of the tide, which set in with unparalleled height and rapidity, and were suddenly engulphed in the tremendous deluge, whilst piteously imploring assistance from the shore. When they saw that they could not escape the tide, they judiciously placed the boat end-on; but such was the overwhelming power of the torrent, that their feeble bark was incapable of resisting its awful force. One of the boatmen, Thomas Knight, (who had been a faithful and cautious servant at

BEACHLEY HOUSE, OLD PASSAGE.

The Passage House at Beachley, c. 1810. The telegraph was for signalling to the opposite bank of the river.

that ferry for eighteen years,) has left a family of seven children; the other, Thomas Rooke, has left three small children; and each of them a pregnant widow, in such circumstances of distress as to render them great objects of charity. Mr. Hewlett (the passenger) had been married but a few weeks.

229   *19 February 1810*

Thatcher and Pritchard beg leave to acquaint the Public, that the times of Crossing at the Old Passage are for five hours on the Flood Tide, if the Wind be to the North or East; and for seven hours on the Ebb Tide, the Wind at South or West. The Crossing is made in as short a time as at the New Passage.

A Dispatch Boat has been established for the convenience of the Public, which crosses when no other Boat can, at the same price as the large Boat.

T. and P. have fitted up their respective Houses with good Accomodations – have excellent Stables, and Post Chaises with Careful Drivers.

N.B. The Hereford Coach passes to and from Bristol every other day, (Sunday excepted.)

230   *11 May 1812*

Melancholy Accident. On Thursday last, as the ferry-boat was crossing the River Severn, at Framilode-Passage, deeply laden with cattle, coming from Ross fair, she unfortunately shipped some water, filled, and sunk about half way over, at the depth of ten feet. The cattle swam for different parts of the shore. The drover who had them in charge, and two boatmen, were the only persons on board: one of the latter supported himself upon a plank; the other mounted one of the horses, but being a stout, powerful man, the animal sunk under him, when he sustained himself by swimming, till boats from the shore picked him and his companion up. But their unhappy passenger perished . . .

231   *20 January 1812*

(in a notice of sale of the Red Lion inn at Arlingham)

This Inn lies upon the great road which will communicate with the intended Tunnel under the Severn, which goes on with great rapidity at present, and nearly one half completed; from the entrance into which, it is distant 1 mile, 16 to Monmouth, 16 to Chepstow, 13 to Ross, 12 to Stroud, 14 to Hampton, 15 to Kingscote, and 13 to Newport; and when that grand Tunnel is completed, it is presumed that the increase of Travelling will render this Inn an eligible situation for a man of spirit, desirous of embarking in the Public Business.

The New Passage, c. 1793, with the passage boat preparing to leave from the Redwick side.

We are sorry to learn, that on Friday morning, about four o'clock, the miners employed in excavating the Tunnel under the River Severn, at Newnham, discovered a small breach, through which the water issued. This for a moment they conceived was occasioned by a spring; but the aperture increasing, they were instantly aware of their danger, and had barely time to be drawn up before the water filled the tunnel. This public-spirited undertaking was completed to the extent of 226 yards, of the breadth of 12 feet, and 13 feet high; and, we trust, the present accident will be productive of no other ill consequence than a temporary suspension of the work.

Index of Places and Subjects

N.B. Non-italic figures are references to the numbers of the newspaper extracts; italic figures are page numbers and refer to the author's commentary or to illustrations. Persons (a selection) are indexed under 'carriers', 'coach proprietors', 'innkeepers', and 'surveyors'.

Abergavenny (Mon.), 3, 66, 80, 116
Abingdon (Berks.), 83, 89, 92, 103, 110; *59*
Ablington, *see* Bibury
Andoversford, 41–2; *33, 46*
Arlingham, 231; *137*
Ashleworth, *137*
Aust, 218; *137, 140*
Avening, *72*

Badminton, 59
Barnsley (Glos.), 25; *25, 104, 106*
Bath, 71, 80–81, 101, 144–5; *97*
  roads to, 43–8, 186; *34–5*
Beachley (in Tidenham), passage (the Old Passage), 217–20, 223, 225, 229; *137–8, 144*
Beechpike (in Winstone), *25*
Benson (Oxon.), *41*
Bibury, *152*
  Ablington, *212*
Birdlip (in Brimpsfield), 193; *1, 25*
Birmingham, 67, 72, 80, 101; *97*
Bisley, 102, 117, 120, 186, 194
Blakeney (in Awre), 40; *138*
Brecon (Brecknock), 8, 66, 80, 109, 116, 213; *44*
bridges, 14; *3–5, 8, 44, 46*
Bristol, 2, 186, 197, 217, 221; *2*
  carriers, 97, 100–1, 103, 119–20; *69, 81*
  coaches, 64, 67, 69, 72, 78, 80, 205, 229; *25–6, 45, 59*
  stone trade, 17, 23; *5, 18*
Burford (Oxon.), 36, 41–2, 71, 75, 107, 116, 177, 207, 210
Buscot (Berks.), 128

Cainscross, *see* Stroud
Cam, 166
Cambridge (in Slimbridge), 55
Campden, Chipping, 100
Carmarthen, 7, 70, 79–80, 116; *97, 138*
carriers, 26, 97–138, 127; *69–70, 76, 78–81, 86, 89–91*
carriers (named):
  Arnold, Rob, 98; *45*
  Ball, Moses, 118
  Ballard, Dan., 119
    Mic., 117

Baylis, A.K., *79*
Chambers, J., 107
Creed, fam., *79*
Gardiner, Thos., 120; *81*
Gill, Wm., 108
Good, Wm, 104; *69*
Heane, Jas., 116
  Rowland, 109, 112, 129; *70*
  fam., *79*
Jones, J., 107
Lewis, Wm., 114
Leyes, John, 105
Madocke, Thos., 97
Manning, Sam., 103; *70*
Masters, Dan., 113
  Thos., *70*
Mountain, Wm., 102
Niblett, Dan. (fl. *c*. 1750), 117
  Dan. (fl. 1796), 123
  John, 122–3
North, Messrs., 109, 116
Restell, John, 101
Shipton, Thos., 118
  fam., *79*
Simpson, John, 110–11
Sirrell, W., 127
Tanner, Sam., 124; *79*
  Tanner and Baylis, 208, 133; *70, 79–80*
Wood, John, 98,
Yeates, Thos., 135
Chalford, 102, 120, 124, 186; *3*
cheese trade, 128–9; *85*
Cheltenham, 152, 177; *14, 24*
  carriers, 102, 116; *79–80*
  coaches, 75, 80, 207; *33, 46, 52*
  inns, 31, 50, 107, 153; *24*
  roads to, 12, 22; *5, 25, 35*
Chepstow (Mon.), 17, 70, 80, 224
Churcham, *96*
Cirencester, 139, 146, 175–7, 199; *32, 97*
  carriers, 102, 110, 113, 117, 127; *70*
  coaches, 65, 71, 89–93, 96, 121; *44, 46, 58, 62*
  highway robberies near, 186, 188, 191, 193
  inns, 90, 96, 176; *21, 28, 32*
  roads to, 10, 19; *1, 25*
Cleeve, Bishop's, *69*

cloth industry, 121–2, 124, 148, 154; *79, 81, 97*
coach proprietors:
 Biggs, Edw., 65
 Garmston, Thos., 67
 Haines, Thos., *52*
 Harris, John, 61–3
  Wm., 82
 Haynes, Wm., 61
 Heath, John, 75, 77
 Hinks, G., 69
 How, Thos., 64
 Jane, T., 69
 Jones, T., 69
 Kemp, Jas., 65
 Masters, fam., *62 and see* Willan
 Neyler, Jas., *79*
 Pain, J., 69, 82
 Phillpotts, John, 70; *58*
 Postan, G., 69
 Pruen, Thos., 198; *33*
 Simkins, Wm., *45*
 Spencer, John, 77, 80; *46*
 Sperinck, Jos., 71
 Thompson, Isaac, 82
 Turner, John, 66–8, 106, 198; *33, 44*
  Wm., 68
 Weeks, J., 69
 Willan, John, 75
  Willan and Co., 77
  Willan, Masters and Co., 90, 93, 96
 Williams, Jas., 82
  R., 75
 Wilts, Thos., 67
 Wimble, Jas., 64
 Winston, Thos., *45*
coaches, 61–96, 121, 213–15; *21, 25–6, 47–7, 52, 79, 132*
 accidents, 198, 202, 205, 207; *127*
 coachmen, character of, 77, 84, 205; *47*
 mail coaches, 81–8, 96, 205, 215; *57–9, 137*
 rivalry, 72, 76, 78, 89–96, 198, 207; *46, 62–3*
coal trade, 16, 27, 33, 99; *23, 69–70*
Cock Road (in Kingswood, near Bristol), 197
Codrington, 1
Cold Harbour, *see* Kingscote
Coleford, 11, 15, 29, 102, 116

Didmarton, 119
Dowdeswell, 12
drovers, Welsh, 27, 171; *23, 25, 104, 106*
Dunkirk, *see* Hawkesbury
Dursley, 116, 118, 124; *79*

Eastington (near Stroud), 120, 124; *34*
Edgeworth, 187
Evesham (Worcs.), 5

Fairford, 89, 92, 102–3, 110–11, 117, 127, 211
fairs, 119, 139, 143, 164–5, 170, 183, 185–6, 201, 230; *96–7, 115*
Falfield, 30
Faringdon (Berks.), 89, 92, 102–3, 110, 117

ferries, *see* passages
fish trade, 106
Flaxley, 200
Framilode (in Fretherne and Saul), 33; *23*
 passage, 230; *137–8*
Frocester, 6, 43–8; *3, 34–5*
Frogmill (in Shipton Solers), 12, 41-2, 58; *33, 46*
Frome (Som.), 134

gipsies, 155–6, 172; *104*
Gloucester, 138, 140–2, 144–6, 174, 188; *4, 84–5, 91, 97, 112, 122, 124, 134, 138*
 carriers, 97–8, 103–4, 109–10, 112, 114, 116, 119–20, 127; *45–6, 70, 79–80, 86*
 coaches, 61–4, 67–70, 73, 75–6, 78–80, 198, 202, 207; *44–6*
  mail coaches, 82, 85–8; *58*
 fairs, 164–5, 170, 183, 185, 192, 201; *104, 127*
 inns, 26–7, 51, 54–5, 57, 64, 101, 103–4, 151, 178–80; *23, 41, 104, 128*
  Bell, 46, 53, 55, 60, 70, 167, 181; *21–3, 41, 58, 104*
  Boothall, 36, 75, 80, 174; *46*
  King's Head, 54, 82; *21, 41, 58*
 roads to, 8–9, 11, 15, 43–8, 130; *1–2, 6, 25, 34, 44, 59, 84*
 robberies near, 189–90, 195–6
 wharfingers, 110, 125–6, 128
Gloucester Journal, 150, 209, 214; *6, 97, 100, 139*
Guiting Power, 171

Hartpury, 201; *127*
 Woolridge, 192
Haw, the (in Tirley), *5, 46, 137*
Hawkesbury:
 Dunkirk, 186
 Petty France, 43, 186
Hereford, 80, 116, 152, 229
 carriers, 26, 127; *69*
 roads to, 8, 135; *1–2, 5, 46*
highwaymen, footpads, etc., 164, 186–97; *104, 121–2*
Horsley, 19, 118, 160, 120; *79*
 Tiltups Inn, 44–5; *25*
Huntley, 102

innkeepers, 49–61; *6, 21, 23, 40–1*
innkeepers (named):
 Adams, Francis, 53
 Cole, Chas., 55
  Thos., 27
 Coleman, Chris., 47
 Collier, John, 41
 Cooke, Josias, 31
 Cosham, Thos., 161; *104*
 Countze, Chas., 59
 Cowles, Geo., 26
 Cullis, Mary, 33
 Dubberley, Wm., 61
 Edmonds, Dan., 221-2
 Elderton, Jas., 46
 Evans, Jas., 55

Field, Dan., *33*
Fricker, Mark, 60
Gomm, John, 153
Graham, Jas., 15
Greenaway, Giles, *21*
Greening, Hen., 56
Hall, Ric., 33; *23*
Harris, Sam., 49
Harvey, Thos., 50
Heath, John, 54
Hill, Sam., 218–19
  Wm., 57
How, Thos., 64
Howes, John, 58
Humphreys, Thos., 42
King, E., 48; *41*
Lane, Jas., 39
Lewis, Eliz., 35
Morse, Wm., 60
Neyler, Jas., 79
Nott, Jas., 51; *41*
Ody, Wm., 28
Phillpotts, John, 47, 70, 167; *21*
Pierce, Thos., *140*
Pritchard, —, 229
Restell, John, 101
Ridler, John, 37
  R., 151
Savage, Jas., 34
Skillin, Thos., 25
Spencer, John, 80
Stratford, Jos., 52
Thatcher, —, 229
Tibbs, Jos., 32
Weaver, John, *28*
  Ric., *28*
Wiltshire, Mrs., 24
Wimble, Jas., 64
inns, *passim, but particularly*, 24–61, 151, 153; *21–6, 28, 31, 33–5, 40–1, 64, 97, 128*
  passage houses, 218, 221, 227, 229; *137, 140, 144*

Kemble, 163
Kilkenny (in Withington), 36,
Kingscote, 61, 96, 152; *79*
  Cold Harbour, 49

Lancaut, 203; *127*
Lechlade, 14, 89, 92, 102–3, 110, 117; *3, 8*
  London traffic, 125–9; *84–5*
Ledbury (Herefs.), 8, 98, 104, 116; *6*
Leicester, 76
Leigh, 173
London, *64, 97*
  carriers, 98, 102–3, 106–7, 109–10, 116–18, 122–4; *45, 69–70, 79, 87*
  coaches, 61–3, 65–6, 68, 75, 79–80, 89–96, 121, 198, 202, 207, 215; *46, 58, 62–3, 138*
  roads to, 25, 130, 135; *1, 5, 25*

mail coaches, *see* coaches
Malmesbury (Wilts.), 118; *79*

markets, 143, 196, 201, 210, 212; *69, 97, 127*
Milford Haven (Pembs.), 79, 88, 116; *44, 59*
Minchinhampton (Hampton, Hampton Road), 19, 89–90, 92, 162, 188; *3, 6, 122*
  carriers, 102–3, 117, 119–20
Mitcheldean, 11, 102, 116, 157; *23*
  inns, 15, 32; *6, 23*
Monmouth, 8, 11, 15, 26, 32, 80, 102, 116

Nailsworth, 19, 43–4, 89, 92, 120, 124; *6, 34–5*
navvies, 6, 160–1; *104–5*
New Barn (in Farmington), 107
New Passage, *see* Redwick
Newent, 18, 80, 104
Newnham, 20, 80, 168, 232; *3*
  passage, 221–2, 228; *137–9*
Newport (in Berkley), 24, 39, 64, 101; *25–6*
newsmen, 51, 150, 209, 214; *41, 97, 134*
Northleach, 36, 75, 156, 212, 116
Nympsfield, 47

Old Passage, *see* Beachley
Oxford, 41–2, 107, 130, 147, 180
  coaches, 61–2, 71, 75, 80, 82
  inns, 36, 61, 71, 107

packhorses, 97, 99, 101, 104; *4, 69, 72*
Painswick, 22, 56, 143, 182, 195; *97*
  carriers, 103, 116–17, 119–20, 124
  Sheepscombe, 108
passages (ferries), 216–30; *137–9*
pedlars, 149; *96*
Perrot's Brook (in Bagendon), 25, 28; *23, 25*
Pershore, *5*
Petty France, *see* Hawkesbury
poor–law system, 158, 160, 163, 173; *105*
postboys, 211, 213
posting, 8–9, 32, 34, 36, 39; *21*
press gang, 140
Preston (near Cirencester), 184
Purton (in Berkley), *137–8*
Purton (in Lydney), 115
  passage, 216, 224, 227; *137–8*

race meetings, 146, 152, 174; *23, 97, 115*
Ready Token (in Poulton), 25; *25*
recruiting officers, 159, 162; *105*
Redwick (in Henbury), passage (the New Passage), 219, 226; *137–8, 146*
riots (against turnpikes), 1–2; *2*
road accidents, 198–208; *127*
'road clubs', 3–4; *5*
roads, improvement of, 1–22, 43–8; *1–3, 5–7*
Rodborough, 19, 158
  carriers, 119–20, 123–4; *79*
  Fleece inn, 43, 45–6, 48; *34–5, 41*
Rodley (in Westbury on Severn), *137*
Ross-on-Wye (Herefs.), 3, 8, 11, 80, 116, 127, 230
  inns, 9, 62; *6, 41*
Ruscombe, *see* Stroud

St. Pierre (Mon.), *137*

150

salesmen, travelling, 148, 151, 153–4; *97*
Salisbury, 119; *81, 97*
Sandhurst, 164
  Wallsworth, 196
Severn (river):
  floods, 213–14; *134*
  passages, 216–30; *137–9*
  trade on, 33, 100, 125; *5, 23, 69, 85*
Sheepscombe, *see* Painswick
Sheperdine (in Rockhampton), *137*
showmen, travelling, 174–85; *115*
Shrewsbury, 80
Sodbury, Chipping, 10, 119–20
Stanley, Leonard, 60
Stonehouse, 120
stone trade, 17, 23; *5, 18*
Stourbridge (Worcs.), 33, 161; *97, 104*
Stow-on-the-Wold, 42, 53, 139, 211; *1*
Stroud (Stroudwater), 159, 181–2, 128, 194; *79, 81*
  Cainscross, 120, 124, 161; *104*
  carriers, 103, 117, 119–20, 124
  coaches, 89–96, 121; *58, 62–3*
  inns, 38, 89–90, 92–3, 95–6, 147, 181
  roads to, 19, 22; *3, 5*
  Ruscombe, 114
Stroudwater canal, 161; *104*
surveyors:
  Hall, R., 44–5
  Parry, Jos., 6
  Pinnell, Thos., 11
Swansea, 80
swindlers, 157, 165–7, 169–70; *104*

Taunton (Som.), *97*
Tenby (Carms.), 33, 80

Tetbury, 6, 13, 34, 172, 182, 186; *1, 3, 96*
  carriers, 103, 118–20; *79*
  coaches, 71, 90, 96, 121; *58*
Tewkesbury, 80, 173, 214; *21, 46, 69–70, 90, 137*
  carriers, 101, 105, 107, 116
  inns, 37, 101, 107; *21, 36*
  roads to, 21, 37; *5*
Thames (river), 14, 125–9; *3, 85*
Thornbury, 52
timber, carriage of, 115; *70, 90*
turnpike gates, 1–2, 5, 13; *2, 4, 14*
turnpike trusts, 5–6, 10–12, 14, 17–22, 43–8, 130–8;
  1–3, 5–7, 89, 91

Uley, 116, 124

Wales, *134, 137*
  carriers in, 102, 109, 116
  coaches in, 66, 70, 79–80, 88; *44, 59*
  drovers from, 27, 171; *23, 25, 104, 106*
  roads in, 3, 7, 66
Wallsworth, *see* Sandhurst
weighing-machines, 134, 136, 138; *91*
Weyhill (Hants.), 139; *97*
Wheatenhurst (or Whitminster), 35, 52; *2, 23*
Winchcombe, *5*
Witney (Oxon.), 71, 75, 107
Woodchester, 19, 89, 120
Woolridge, *see* Hartpury
Worcester, 67, 80, 97, 101, 103–4, 141, 146
Wotton-under-Edge, 96, 118, 124; *79*

Yate, 2